PYTHON

PYTHON BASICS FOR BEGINNERS

Andy Vickler

© Copyright 2021 - All rights reserved.

In no way is it legal to reproduce, duplicate, or transmit any part of this document in either electronic means or in printed format. Recording of this publication is strictly prohibited and any storage of this document is not allowed unless with written permission from the publisher. All rights reserved.

The information provided herein is stated to be truthful and consistent, in that any liability, in terms of inattention or otherwise, by any usage or abuse of any policies, processes, or directions contained within is the solitary and utter responsibility of the recipient reader. Under no circumstances will any legal responsibility or blame be held against the publisher for any reparation, damages, or monetary loss due to the information herein, either directly or indirectly.

Respective authors own all copyrights not held by the publisher.

Legal Notice:

This ebook is copyright protected. This is only for personal use. You cannot amend, distribute, sell, use, quote or paraphrase any part or the content within this ebook without the consent of the author or copyright owner. Legal action will be pursued if this is breached.

Disclaimer Notice:

Please note the information contained within this document is for educational and entertainment purposes only. Every attempt has been made to provide accurate, up to date and reliable complete information. No warranties of any kind are expressed or implied. Readers acknowledge that the author is not engaging in the rendering of legal, financial, medical or professional advice.

By reading this document, the reader agrees that under no circumstances are we responsible for any losses, direct or indirect, which are incurred as a result of the use of information contained within this document, including, but not limited to, —errors, omissions, or inaccuracies.

Table of Contents

Introduction 1

Chapter One: A Brief History of Python 3
    Python's First Release 4
    Python 3.0 6
    The Future 7
    How to Install Python 8
    Installing Python Windows 10 8
    Installing Python on Mac OS 12
    Installing Python on Linux 14
    Troubleshooting Installation Problems 15

Chapter Two: Python Datatypes 16
    Python Variables 17
    Naming Variables 18
    Python Datatypes 21
    Strings 23
    String Concatenation 25
    Whitespaces 26
    Stripping Whitespace 27
    Syntax Errors 28
    Numbers 29

The Zen of Python 33

Chapter Three: Python Lists 35

Defining Lists 35

Accessing Elements 36

List Modification 40

Remove() Method 47

List Organization 49

Sorted() Function 50

List Length 52

Looping Through Lists 53

Indentation 59

Post-Loop Unnecessary Indentation 61

Numerical Lists 62

List Slicing 65

Copying Lists 67

Chapter Four: Python Tuples 71

Length 72

Changing Elements 73

Creating Loop 74

Overwriting a Tuple 74

Code Styling 76

Chapter Five: Python Conditionals 79

Numerical Testing 83

Testing Multiple Conditions 84

The if Statement 87

if-else Statements 88

    The if-elif-else Chain 89

    Multiple elif Statements 92

    Omitting else Block 94

    Multiple Conditions 95

    If Statement & Lists 96

    Special Items 97

Chapter Six: Python Dictionaries 102

    A Dictionary 103

    Accessing Values 104

    Empty Dictionary 106

    Modification 107

    Key-Pair Removal 108

    Looping a Dictionary 111

    Nesting 119

    Dictionary & Lists 123

Chapter Seven: User Input & While Loops 130

    Input() Function 131

    While Loops 135

    Quit Button 136

    Flag 139

    Break Statement 141

    Continue Statement 143

    While Loops, Lists & Dictionaries 143

    Removing Instances 145

    Filling Up Dictionaries 146

Chapter Eight: Python Functions **148**
    Arguments & Parameters 150
    Default Values 153

Chapter Nine: Classes **158**
    Creating Eagle Class 158

Conclusion **162**

References **163**

Introduction

This book on Python's basics contains proven steps and strategies on how to be master the basics of Python programming. I recommend that you keep your laptop open in front of you while reading this book. This book is more practical than theoretical. It will challenge you to try coding yourself. It is easy enough for any beginner to start coding right away.

I have given functional codes in the book and comprehensive explanations to avoid any difficulty when practicing the codes.

There is no prior knowledge of Python required to read the book. I started the book from the basics and took it over to object-oriented programming, which falls into the advanced level domain. I just touched the concept slightly to give you a flavor of how you can use Python in the practical world.

With a good grasp of the Python basics, you can automate simple tasks, which can help you with simple home or work chores. After mastering the basics, you can use them to build machine learning models. Different Python libraries like Keras and TensorFlow can help you build Artificial Intelligence and Machine Learning models. Both are in demand and are highly useful in solving real-life problems. For example, artificial intelligence models can power robotic machines, customer services centers, retail outlets, the health sector for diagnosing diseases, etc.

The applications of Python are endless. Artificial Intelligence systems tend to learn from the data that you feed to them. This is similar to the human brain. Machine learning models also work on data. Although they are not as efficient as artificial intelligence models, they also have wider applications. They are used in the manufacturing industry where human labor cannot work. They can handle bigger robotic machines and wrap up complicated tasks in a simple and fast manner.

I hope you enjoy your codes and the time you will spend on debugging your codes as well. Please don't forget to keep a notebook and a pen by your side. Best of luck to you for your reading ventures!

Chapter One

A Brief History of Python

Python is a programming language that is highly focused on bringing ease to the users and simplicity to the programmers at the beginner's level. It allows programmers to write the code in structural, object-oriented, and functional styles. It is presently widely used in several fields like machine learning and developing websites. After the highly famous and used JavaScript, Python is the second most used programming language worldwide.

The founder and creator of Python is Guido van Rossum. Until 2018, he played a key role in the development of Python, making decisions that would affect the changes and the updates to the programming language.

In 1989, he was working on a microkernel-based system called Amoeba. For that system, he developed certain system utilities. While he was working on them, he realized that program development in C used to consume too much time and energy. He decided that he would spend his free time building a dedicated language to help him finish his work quickly.

He hit upon an idea to script a language that would fall somewhere between the shell script and C in terms of functionality and nature. Simply put, he wanted an interpreted language. However, he also wanted it to be easily programmable and readable compared to shell scripts.

Therefore, he developed Python. As the popular belief might be, Python is in no way named after the poisonous snake species. It is named after a British comedy troupe, namely Monty Python.

The word Python also turned out to be catchy and eye-popping. Not only is it a bit edgy, but it also fulfills the tradition of choosing saucy names and naming after highly famous people.

Python's First Release

The language Python was first released at the institute at which Guido had been working. He agreed with the manager to publish Python as an open-source language.

In February 1991, Van Rossum published the source code for the interpreter of Python to alt.sources. Nowadays, almost all programming languages are open-source and can be easily traced on GitHub. At the point of the release, it was not clear what the business model of the people who were developing those languages would be.

There were different proprietary languages, but it was a bit difficult for them to gain popularity. Guido knew that the idea of open-sourcing was the only viable way to make Python a success.

Sharing the open-source code was never easy. Originally, the developers faced some difficulties. They had to split up the source code for the Python interpreter into 21 uuencoded messages for sharing with different newsgroups. The idea worked and proved to be a better replacement for carrying along with a physical version of the source code.

The first release of Python had classes, functions, exception handling, and different core datatypes like str, list, dict, etc. It also was heavily inspired by the ABC language that Guido implemented at CWI. While he was creating Python, his goal was to take up all the good parts of ABC and fix the rest of them. In January 1994, he released the 1.0 version, and a milestone in the history of Python was achieved.

At that time, the market also welcomed many other interpreted languages similar to Python, two of them being Ruby and Perl. This shows that the market definitely needed an easily interpreted language.

The US National Institute for Standards and Technology invited Guido in 1994. NIST was interested in the use of Python for many standards-related projects. They also needed somebody to boost Python skills, so they decided to get Guido, the creator of Python, onboard.

With the support of NIST, Guido could run several workshops and would participate in different conferences. He managed to spread Python and attract certain key contributors that would play an important role in shaping the future of this new programming language.

This resulted in different job offers for Guido from CNRI that was a non-profit research laboratory. This specific position helped Guido gather a team of enthusiastic people who would later support him to release Python versions.

The Python language started shaping up nicely with perfect principles and priorities. A fine example of the principles of Python is Python's Zen, a certain set of aphorisms from a software engineer, namely Tom Peters. The Zen carries Python's core philosophy.

In 1996, the Python language was used to build different products such as Microsoft Server, a part of Windows NT. Python 2.0 that was released in October 2000, brought list comprehensions. List comprehensions are a common Python feature present in several programming languages such as Haskell. It also added many features like Unicode support and a garbage can. Python was gradually inching toward the future as a reliable language with comfortable development experience.

Python 3.0

Starting from the year 200, the core developers began thinking about releasing Python 3.0. They desired to streamline different languages like cutting unnecessary language functions and constructs that Python sought to accrue in around 20 years. Their efforts resulted in Python 3.0, a backward-incompatible version of the Python language that came out in 2008. However, the release of the language was not as smooth as it was thought to be. It was filled up with several complications.

The developers did not realize how much Python code depended on the libraries of Python. So, while it was really easy to shift your scripts to Python 3, it was harder to move the programs that relied on the third-party libraries since they could not upgrade fast.

While Python was growing steadily, from 2010, it began on the trajectory of growth that enabled it to compete with top computer programming languages, such as JavaScript and Java.

With exponential growth in machine learning, a rise in the number of developers, and big data, the popularity of Python shot to the sky. The machine learning journey of Python got to the inflection point around September 2016 as per Google Trends, following the release of TensorFlow. This also is similar to the rise in the worldwide interest in the field of machine learning.

The Future

In the future of Python frameworks like Flask and Django, it is a great option for simple and quick web development. Python enjoys top support for machine learning programs across different programming languages because of its heavyweight libraries such as Keras and TensorFlow. The easy syntax makes it the best programming language of choice for data scientists and ML experts.

Python is equipped with some wonderful tools to do data analysis and visualization, making it the best choice at different points in the data pipeline. One of the best things you should know about Python is that it enables specialists in different domains to start quick programming. The popularity of Python is gradually growing because it is highly versatile and applicable to different fields that are boosted with the help of automation, big data, and machine learning. This makes Python one of the most popular programming languages.

How to Install Python

Python is considered the most widely used programming language. It has gained popularity and is also considered one of the most flexible and highly popular server-side programming languages. Unlike most of the distributions of Linux, Windows does not have any pre-installed version of Python. However, you can install it on your local machine or Windows server in a few easy steps.

Installing Python Windows 10

There are some prerequisites to installing Python on your system. The first is a system that has Windows 10 installed on it. You also should have admin privileges. The second prerequisite is the command prompt that comes with Windows by default. The third prerequisite is a remote desktop app. You can use it if you are about to install Python on a remote Windows server.

Step 1

The first step is downloading the official Python .exe installer. After you have installed it, you need to run it on your system. The version depends on what you need to do with Python. If you have been working on a certain project coded in Python version 2.6, you might need this version. If you are just starting a project from scratch, you have the freedom to choose.

I recommend that if you are learning coding in Python, you should look out for the latest version of Python to enjoy the latest features. However, if you have any older test projects stored on your system, you may opt for downloading Python 2 to have backward compatibility for those older projects. Python offers Remote Desktop Protocol (RDP) as well. Once you log into the remote server, you have to follow the same installation process to install it on a local Windows system.

Step 2

To complete the second step, open up your web browser. Go to python.org. Once you are on the website, find the Download Python for Windows button. You will find multiple versions of Python on the website. Download the one that suits you. You can either download the x86 or 64 or the x86 installer. Choose and click.

If you are running 32-bit Windows, you should download the x86 installer. Otherwise, download the x-86-64 installer. If, by mistake, you install the wrong version, uninstall it and then reinstall the right version.

Step 3

Now that you have downloaded the installer, you should run it. It will install Python on your system. Make sure to add Python to the path and enable Python for all users on the system. Adding Python to the path allows the interpreter to access the execution path.

Now select *Install Now*.

For all the versions of Python, the options for recommended installation include IDLE and Pip. The older versions may not include any additional features.

The next dialog box will ask you to disable the path length limit. Disabling it will help Python use lengthy path names. The disable path length limit option does not affect the other system settings. If you turn it on, it will resolve the issues regarding name length that pop up in Python projects developed in Linux.

When you have installed Python, you can go to the Start Menu on your Windows or click on the Windows sign to search where Python is located. Find it and run Python IDLE. I have got Python 3 on my computer system. When I run it for the first time, here is what I see on the screen.

```
Python 3.8.5 (tags/v3.8.5:580fbb0, Jul 20
2020, 15:57:54) [MSC v.1924 64 bit (AMD64)]
on win32
Type "help", "copyright", "credits" or
"license()" for more information.
>>>
```

Step 4

Now you need to verify whether Python is successfully and properly installed on Windows or not. You need to navigate to the directory where you have installed Python on your system. Double-click python.exe. You will see the installed version of Python. You also can check if the installation had been successful by typing –V in the Command Prompt.

Step 5

The next step is to verify whether Pip was installed on the system or not. If you opted to install the older version of Python, it might not come with a preinstalled Pip. Pip is an extremely powerful package management system to create software packages in Python, so make sure it is installed. I recommend that you use Pip for different Python packages when you are working inside certain virtual environments.

For verification of Pip, you need to do the following:

1. First of all, you need to open the Start menu and enter 'cmd.'

2. You need to open the Command Prompt application.

3. Enter pip –V inside the console. The output will verify whether Pip was installed on your system or not.

Step 6

You need to open the Start menu and then initiate the Run app. Here, type sysdm.cpl and then click OK. This will open the System

Properties window. Now navigate to the Advanced lab and then select the Path variable. Now click Edit. Here you need to select the Variable value field. At this point, you can add path to the python.exe file that is preceded with a semicolon(;).

Click Ok and shut down all the windows. When you have set it up, you can execute certain Python scripts such as Python script.py. This script is cleaner and can be easily managed.

Step 7

Now you have installed Python and Pip to manage different packages, you only need one final software package - virtualnv. It will enable you to create certain isolated local virtual environments for several Python projects.

Python software packages come pre-installed by default. As a result, whenever any specific package faces change, it tends to change for all the Python projects. You may need to avoid this. Having separate virtual environments for different projects probably is the easiest solution you can have.

For installing virtualnv, you need to open the Start menu and type "cmd." Then you need to select the Command Prompt application. After that, you should type the pip command inside the console. When it is completed, virtualnv is installed on your system.

Installing Python on Mac OS

The recommended approach on macOS is to install Python using the official installer at Python.org. Previously, Homebrew's package manager was the recommended option because it made installations and updates easy in most cases. However, it doesn't work too well anymore for Python, so Homebrew is the best option.

Step 1

Opening your browser, go to www.python.org/downloads and click the button to download the latest version of Python.

Step 2

A popup message will ask if you want to allow the site to download; click Yes. Then open a Finder window and click Downloads on the sidebar. Double-click the Python package to start the installation.

The Python Installer opens, click the Continue button.

On the Read Me page, click on Continue and then click Continue on the Licence page. This will bring up another popup, asking you to agree to the terms and conditions. Click on Agree.

Click Install on the next screen, and Python will be saved to your hard drive.

Enter the password when asked for it and click on Install Software.

Click Close on the Summary window, and a new popup will ask you if you want the installer placed in your trash bin. Click Move to Trash because you don't need it anymore.

A new Finder window will also open, showing you the Python package you just installed.

Click the link for IDLE, as this is the easiest way to use Python. A new Shell opens where you can type your commands. You can also use the command line to access Python. Open Applications>Utilities>Terminal and type python3 – the interpreter will open, and if you see the command prompt - >>> - it is working properly.

Installing Python on Linux

Most of today's Linux distributions have Python already installed by default. To check your current version, open the terminal and run the command below. Do not include the $ (dollar sign) as this is the command prompt:

```
$ python --version
Python 3.9.5
```

If your version comes up as 2.xxx, repeat the above command using python3:

```
$ python3 --version
Python 3.9.5
```

At the time of writing, v3.9 is the most up-to-date Python version, but anything from 3.6 onwards will be good enough.

Linux provides a lot of different installation options, but the easiest one to use is called deadsnakes. Open your terminal and enter these commands:

```
$ sudo add-apt-repository ppa:deadsnakes/ppa
$ sudo apt-get update
$ sudo apt install python3.9
```

Python 3.9 will be installed, and you can start a new session by typing the following at the command prompt:

```
$ python3.9
>>>
```

Troubleshooting Installation Problems

I hope that your installation venture is successful on the first attempt. However, if you are unable to do that, you may need to fix some installation problems. Here are a few remedies you may try.

When a certain program contains a prominent error, Python will display a traceback error. Python will look through the file and then try to report the problem. The traceback might offer you a clue as to what is wrong with the code and what prevents your program from running.

The best practice is to step away from your computer for a while. Take a break and try again. Syntax is extremely important in the world of programming, so even if there is a missing colon, mismatched parentheses, or a mismatched quotation mark, it will prevent your program from running properly. You should reread all the parts of the code, look at what you have done, and remove any errors.

Chapter Two

Python Datatypes

This chapter will walk you through various types of data that you can work with to create your Python programs. You will learn how you can store data inside different variables, and you will also learn how you can use these variables inside the programs. Variables can be defined as containers that are used to store different values. You can, when the need arises, use these variables to perform different tasks. Let's write the first code in Python. I will write a print statement that will display what I will write in the code.

```
print("I am learning Python from scratch.")
I am learning Python from scratch.
```

I wrote the code with the print command in Python editor. You can open this editor by clicking on the File in the menu line and then New. A new Editor window will pop up on your screen. You can start writing code here. The output that you can see after the demarcating line is displayed in the IDLE.

The editor runs the file through a Python interpreter or IDLE in simple words. The interpreter reads through the Python program and then determines what each word in the editor means. When the editor finds the word print, it prints whatever exists in the parentheses that follow the print keyword.

As you write programs, the editor will highlight different parts of the program in several ways. For example, it will recognize that the print keyword is the name of a Python function. That's why you will see that the word print will appear in blue. It will immediately display the statement in the parenthesis. The coloring feature of Python is known as syntax highlighting. This feature is very useful, especially when you begin writing your programs.

Python Variables

In the following section, I will explain how you can use Python variables. You can add a new line at the start of the file and then modify the second line. See how I will do that.

```
mg1 = ("Python is an easy and interpreted language.")
print(mg1)
Python is an easy and interpreted language.
```

You can see that the output is the same as we had before. So, what is different here? I have added a variable named mg1 in the code. Every variable in Python holds a specific value. This is the information that is associated with the same variable. In this particular case, the value is a statement.

The addition of a variable causes a bit more work for the Python interpreter. When the interpreter processes the first line of code, it tends to associate the text with the message of the variable. When it gets to the second line, it usually prints the value associated with the message toward your computer screen. Let's expand this program by adding more lines of code.

```
mg1 = ("Python is an easy and interpreted
language.")
print(mg1)

mg1 = ("You can learn Python easily by
practice.")
print(mg1)

Python is an easy and interpreted language.
You can learn Python easily by practice.
```

This means that you can always change the value of the variable in your program at any time. Also, Python keeps track of every change in the current value of the variable.

Naming Variables

When you are working on variables in Python, you have to adhere to several guidelines and rules. Breaking these rules will definitely cause certain errors. Different guidelines will help you write code that's easier to understand and read. However, you need to be sure that you follow a set of rules when naming them.

The first rule is that the names of variables should only contain numbers, letters, and underscores. They may start with an underscore and a letter but never with a number. For example, you can write mg1 but not 1mg. You cannot add spaces to the names of variables, but you can use underscores to create separation between words in the names of variables. For example, you can write mg_morning, but you cannot write mg morning. It will trigger an immediate error.

You should also avoid using the reserved keywords of Python and the names of functions to name your variables. For example, you cannot use print, a Python keyword, as a name for a variable.

The names of variables need to be short but highly descriptive. For example, the name student is better than st. A descriptive name helps you understand the code better. You need to be extremely careful about not confusing lowercase l with 1 and uppercase O with 0. Never make this mistake, or your code will never run smoothly.

Just like coding itself, writing a standard variable name also takes some practice. You need to keep the rules and traditions in mind before starting to produce standard names when you practice.

Python variables that you may be using at the moment might be lowercase. If you write uppercase names, you will not see any error. Still, it is a good idea to write names in lower case letters.

If you write a variable name and make a mistake, don't worry because it is normal. Every programmer takes time to grasp the traditions of naming variables. Before they become a naming expert, they make a lot of mistakes. The point is that you must know how to respond to the errors that keep popping up from time to time.

The first error you may make when writing a variable's name is writing the wrong spelling. In the following example, I will write wrong spellings and see what kind of error I will have. See how it is done.

```
mg1 = ("Python is an easy and interpreted language.")
print(msg1)
```

Traceback (most recent call last):

```
    File "C:/Users/saifia computers/Desktop/python.py", line 2, in <module>
        print(msg1)
NameError: name 'msg1' is not defined
>>>
```

The output says that you have incurred an error. It clearly returns that the name msg1 is not defined. By this phrase, you should understand that Python cannot define a variable because it cannot match its name with any in the code. You might have written the wrong name, or the variable does not exist at all. This is a name error. I added an additional letter 's' to the variable's name, which triggered an error. The Python interpreter usually does not spellcheck the code but ensures that the variables' names must be spelled consistently.

Computers disregard good and bad spelling. They only know the spelling that you use for the names of the variables. As a result, you need not consider the grammar rules or English spelling when creating the names of variables or writing the code. Several programming errors are quite simple. They are like single-character typos. Many experienced programmers have to spend hours hunting down these tiny errors to run their code successfully. The best method to understand the new programming concepts is to attempt to use the same when you write your own programs.

Python Datatypes

In the world of programming, the data type is a very important concept. Different data types do different things and Python has different data types to help programmers achieve their programming objectives. Let us explore different data types in the following example.

```
>>> #This is Python string
>>> a = str (" I am learning Python from scratch.")
>>> print(a)
 I am learning Python from scratch.
>>> #This is Python int datatype
>>> a = int(40)
>>> print(a)
40
>>> #This is Python float
>>> a = float(30.777)
>>> print(a)
30.777
#This is Python list
```

```
>>> a = list(("Great expectations", "God of
flies", "God of small things", "Tempest",
"Othello"))
>>> print(a)
['Great expectations', 'God of flies', 'God
of small things', 'Tempest', 'Othello']
>>> #This is Python tuple
>>> a = tuple(("Great expectations", "God of
flies", "God of small things", "Tempest",
"Othello"))
>>> print(a)
('Great expectations', 'God of flies', 'God
of small things', 'Tempest', 'Othello')
>>> #This is Python range
>>> a = range(7)
>>> print(a)
range(0, 7)
>>> #This is Python set
>>> a = set (("Great expectations", "God of
flies", "God of small things", "Tempest",
"Othello"))
>>> print(a)
{'Othello', 'Tempest', 'God of small
things', 'Great expectations', 'God of
flies'}
>>> #This is Python frozenset
>>> a = frozenset(("Great expectations",
"God of flies", "God of small things",
"Tempest", "Othello"))
>>> print(a)
frozenset({'Othello', 'Tempest', 'God of
small things', 'Great expectations', 'God of
flies'})
```

Strings

Most programs gather data or define something. Then they use the same data to produce something useful. It helps in classifying various types of data. The first data type that I will dig into in this section is strings. Strings are simple if you take a look at them. However, when you start using them, they may feel more complicated than you had initially thought.

A simple string usually is a bundle of characters. Anything that is inside the quotes is considered a string. You can either use single or double quotes around the strings like the following.

```
"Python is giving me a tough time to learn."
'Python is giving me a tough time to learn.'
```

This is how you can integrate apostrophes into your code without risking errors to the code. See the following example.

```
'I said to my father, "You will fail if you start losing friends."'
"The programming language 'Python' is the best computer language I ever got to learn."
"My uncle's best habit is that he never stops learning and gaining new knowledge."
```

So, this is how you can use the single and double quotes to your benefit. You can use different string methods to perform some amazing things. See how you can change the case of letters through string methods.

```
mg1 = ("Python is an interpreted language.")
print(mg1.title())
```

```
Python Is An Interpreted Language.
```

In this example, I have taken a lowercase string that was stored in a variable. The method title() that I have included in the code after the print() statement will convert the case of the letters. A method is generally any action that Python performs on a given set of data. The dot (.) that comes after the variable's name in the method tells Python that the title() method acts on the variable's name. Parentheses follow each method in Python because methods often demanded additional information to perform their work. That piece of information is filled up inside the parentheses. The title() function does not require additional information so, the parentheses are generally empty.

The method title() displays all the words in the title case, where each word starts with a capital letter. This is highly useful because you may need to think of a name as an additional piece of information.

Many other useful methods are available to deal with cases. You can switch the string to all lowercase or all uppercase letters such as the following. I will use the same string to apply the uppercase and lowercase methods. See the following example.

```
mg1 = ("Python is an interpreted language.")
print(mg1.upper())
print(mg1.lower())
```

PYTHON IS AN INTERPRETED LANGUAGE.

python is an interpreted language.

The lowercase method is highly useful for storing sets of data. You won't trust the capitalization that the users provide often, so you will have to convert the strings into lowercase before you can store them in the database. When you display information, you will have to use the case that makes the best sense for a string.

String Concatenation

It is highly useful if you start combining strings. For example, you may want to store the first and last name in separate variables. Then you will have to combine them when you have to display the full name of a person.

```
f_name = "John"
l_name = "Wick"
complete_name = f_name + " " + l_name + " " + "is the best action movie."

print(complete_name)

John Wick is the best action movie.
```

Python uses the plus symbol for combining two or more strings. In the above example, I have used the + operator for creating a complete name. The most important thing in this regard is the inclusion of space that you can find between two strings. If we exclude the space between the strings, we will have joined strings that are neither good-looking nor comprehensible.

The method of joining two or more strings through the plus operator is called concatenation. You can use this method for composing messages as I did in the example. Suppose you have a program that demands the first and last name of the users and return greetings when they have given their information to the system.

```
f_name = "John"
l_name = "Wick"
complete_name = "Hello, " + f_name + " " +
l_name + "! How are you doing today?"

print(complete_name)

Hello, John Wick! How are you doing today?
```

Whitespaces

In programming, whitespace means any nonprinting character like tabs, spaces, and end-of-line symbols. You may use whitespace for organizing the output so that it is quite easier for the users to understand.

Let's see how you can add tabs to a piece of text. Here is the character combination \t.

```
print("Python")
print ("\tPython")

Python
    Python
```

If you want to add a newline to the string, you can use the character \n.

```
print ("I can play the following
games:\nCricket\nFootball\nSoccer\nBasketbal
l")
```

I can play the following games:

```
Cricket
Football
Soccer
Basketball
```

You can combine different newlines and tabs into a single string. The string \"\n\" instructs Python to shift to a new line and then start the next line with the help of a new tab. The following example will show how you can use the one-line string for generating different types of output.

Stripping Whitespace

While whitespace is desirable and highly useful in Python programs, it can be confusing in some programs. In programming, the words 'python' and 'python ' may appear to be the same to the programmers but are not to the programs. They are two completely different strings. Python immediately detects the extra space in the second one and considers it of significance unless you instruct it otherwise.

You must consider whitespace as an important section of Python programming because you may come across situations in which you may have to compare two strings to determine if they are inherently the same or not. One important instance may involve checking the usernames of the people when they login to your website. Extra whitespace may turn out to be confusing in simpler situations. Fortunately, Python eases off the elimination of extraneous whitespace from the data that people fill into the program.

Python looks out for extra whitespace to the left and right sides of the string. In order to ensure that there is no whitespace at the right end of the string, you can use the rstrip() method in the code.

Syntax Errors

One most common type of error that you may see in the Python codes with a hint of regularity is a syntax error. A syntax error happens when Python fails to recognize a particular section of a program as the valid Python code. For example, if you use an apostrophe inside the single quotes, you may strike an error. This happens because Python generally interprets everything between the first single quote and apostrophe in the form of a string. After that, it attempts to interpret the remaining piece of text as the Python code. This results in errors.

Here is how you can use single and double quotation marks accurately.

```
best_movie = "Lewis Carrol's Alice In
Wonderland is the best fantasy movie."
print(best_movie)

Lewis Carrol's Alice In Wonderland is the
best fantasy movie.
```

The above program has an apostrophe inside the quotation marks, but there is no problem running them because I have put the apostrophe inside double quotation marks. However, if you use single quotes, Python will not identify at what point the string will end.

```
best_movie = 'Lewis Carrol's Alice In
Wonderland is the best fantasy movie.'
print(best_movie)
```

However, if I run the above-mentioned code, it will trigger a syntax error. This syntax error indicates that the Python interpreter does not recognize the code. Syntax errors are the least specific type of error, which is why they can be hard and frustrating to correct if you are stuck on a stubborn error.

The highlighting feature of the editor will help you find out a bunch of syntax errors fast as you write your programs.

Numbers

You can use numbers quite often when you are programming to add scores to different games. You can also use numbers to represent sets of data in visualizations and store information in different web applications. Python treats different sets of numbers in several ways, depending on how they are used. Let us take a look at how Python handles integers. Integers are the simplest form of numbers in Python.

Integers

You can perform different functions with integers. Here is a summary of them.

```
>>> #Adding integers
>>> 56 + 4
60
>>> #Subtracting numbers
>>> 345 - 45
300
>>> #Subtracting bigger number from smaller number
>>> 345 - 445
-100
>>> # Multiplying numbers
>>> 34 * 45
1530
>>> # Dividing Numbers
>>> 555 / 5
111.0
>>> #Double multiplication
>>> 5 ** 5
3125
>>> 3 ** 2
9
>>> 11 ** 5
161051
>>>
```

Python calls numbers that have a decimal point a float. The term is generally used in several programming languages. A decimal point may appear at a given position inside a number. Each programming language needs to be carefully designed to manage the numbers with points so the numbers behave appropriately regardless of the point the decimal point appears.

For the most part, you may use decimals without worrying about how they tend to behave. You may simply enter all the numbers that you want to use. Python will do what you expect from it.

```
>>> 1.5 + 1.6
3.1
>>> 555.5 - 55.9
499.6
>>> 34.56 * 45.5
1572.48
>>> 34 * 0.8
27.200000000000003
>>> 345 / 5.6
61.60714285714286
>>> 345.5 / 54.6
6.327838827838828
>>>
```

When you are working with datatypes, you are most likely to cause unexpected errors due to the variation in the types of data. For example, you may want to use the value of a variable inside a message. If you are telling someone about the sequel number of the movie, you may need to write the code like the following.

```
sequel = 1
best_movie = "Lewis Carrol's Alice In Wonderland novel has " + sequel + "sequel as well."
print(best_movie)
Traceback (most recent call last):
  File "C:/Users/saifia computers/Desktop/python.py", line 2, in <module>
```

```
        best_movie = "Lewis Carrol's Alice In
Wonderland novel has " + sequel + "sequel as
well."
TypeError: can only concatenate str (not
"int") to str
>>>
```

You can see that the interpreter returned a type error. It means that Python cannot recognize what kind of information you might be using. In the above-mentioned example, Python sees that you have been using a variable that comes with an integer value (int). However, Python does not know how to interpret that value. When you use integers inside strings in this way, you have to specify that Python should use this integer as a string. You can achieve this goal by wrapping up the variable inside the str() function, which instructs Python to represent the non-string values in the form of strings. Here is the right way to write this code.

```
sequel = 1
best_movie = "Lewis Carrol's Alice In
Wonderland novel has " + str(sequel) + "
sequel as well."
print(best_movie)

Lewis Carrol's Alice In Wonderland novel has
1 sequel as well.
```

Working with numbers is the most straightforward thing. However, if you start getting unexpected results, you need to check whether Python interprets the numbers the way you want it to.

The Zen of Python

For many years, the Perl programming language was considered the mainstay of the Internet. Most of the interactive websites in the early days had Perl as a power pack. The moto of the Perl community was to find more than one way to do a task. People loved the approach for some time because the flexibility of the language made it possible to solve complex problems. Ultimately, people realized that the focus on the flexibility factor made it hard to maintain some big projects over a considerably longer period of time. It was tedious, difficult, and extremely time-consuming to review the code and figure out what others had been thinking when solving complex problems.

Experienced programmers of Python would ask you to avoid complexity and use a simple approach wherever possible. The philosophy of Python's community can be traced in the Zen of Python. You can find it out by writing the following code and importing the document.

```
import this

The Zen of Python, by Tim Peters

Beautiful is better than ugly.
Explicit is better than implicit.
Simple is better than complex.
Complex is better than complicated.
Flat is better than nested.
Sparse is better than dense.
```

The document is long. I have just included a few sentences to show you what you will find after running the code in Python editor. Python programmers like the code to be beautiful. It must look elegant. Programmers solve different problems that people face, and they respect efficient, well-designed, and beautiful solutions to different problems. As you start learning more about Python and use it to write more code, the on-looker should praise the beauty of the code.

If you have a choice between a simple and complex solution, try using a simple solution. Even if your code is complex, you should make a conscious effort to make it readable and elegant. When creating a project that involves complex codes, you need to focus on including informative comments to the code.

Your solutions should be compatible and creative. Most programming consists of small and common approaches to fairly simple situations for creating a larger and creative project.

Chapter Three

Python Lists

This chapter will walk you through Python lists. I will explain what lists are and how you can start working with different elements in the list. Python lists allow you to store different sets of information in a centralized place, whether you have one item or one million to deal with. Lists are considered as one of Python's most robust features. They have the power to tie together several important concepts into programming.

Defining Lists

A Python list is, in simple words, a collection of different items that are organized in a specific order. You can create a list that may include different alphabet letters, a set of digits from 0-9, and the names of the people in the family. You can put anything that you want on the list. The items in your list don't have to be related to one another. It is the best way to make your list plural, including letters, names, or digits.

In Python, you can use square brackets to indicate a list. Individual elements in a list are usually separated with the help of commas.

See the following example of a list that consists of different types of guns.

```
guns = ['shotgun', 'pistol', 'revolver',
'bazooka', 'machine gun']
print(guns)
['shotgun', 'pistol', 'revolver', 'bazooka',
'machine gun']
```

Accessing Elements

Lists are highly ordered collections. You can access elements in a list by instructing Python about the position or index of the desired item. You should write the name of the list and then the item's index number inside square brackets. See how I access elements from the list that I have just produced.

```
guns = ['shotgun', 'pistol', 'revolver',
'bazooka', 'machine gun']
print(guns)
print(guns[0])
print(guns[2])
print(guns[4])

['shotgun', 'pistol', 'revolver', 'bazooka',
'machine gun']
shotgun
revolver
machine gun
```

This is the result you will have. You will see a neat and clean formatted output on the interpreter screen. You also can use the string methods that I have already explained in the datatype section to format the output furthermore. Here is what happens when you enter the index number that never exists, like an out-of-range index number.

```
guns = ['shotgun', 'pistol', 'revolver',
'bazooka', 'machine gun']
print(guns[8])
```

Traceback (most recent call last):

```
   File "C:/Users/saifia
computers/Desktop/python.py", line 2, in
<module>
      print(guns[8])
IndexError: list index out of range
```

Python clearly tells you that you have made an index error while writing the code. You also can integrate different string methods in the code like the title(), lower(), or upper() method to alter the formatting of the output.

```
guns = ['shotgun', 'pistol', 'revolver',
'bazooka', 'machine gun']
print(guns[0].title())
print(guns[1].lower())
print(guns[2].upper())
print(guns[3].title())
print(guns[4].upper())

Shotgun
pistol
REVOLVER
Bazooka
MACHINE GUN
```

Another important thing is that Python considers the first item as index 0, not index 1. If you make this mistake and consider it as index 1, the index of the entire list will be affected. Most programming languages have indices that start at 0. Python also offers negative indexing. You can display items from the end of the list by using negative indexing. Negative indexing is different from positive indexing as it starts with -1 and not 0. See how you can use it.

```
guns = ['shotgun', 'pistol', 'revolver',
'bazooka', 'machine gun']
print(guns[-1])
print(guns[-2])
print(guns[-3])
print(guns[-4])
print(guns[-5])

machine gun
bazooka
revolver
pistol
shotgun
```

This syntax is highly useful because sometimes, you need to access the items at the end of the list without knowing the length of the list. As you can see, the first index returns the first item from the end of the list, the second index returns the second item from the end of the list, and the third index returns the third item from the list.

You also can use individual values from the list, just like you would do with other variables. You can use concatenation for creating messages based on the value from the list. Let us see how to use a value from the list and create a message through the same works.

```
guns = ['shotgun', 'pistol', 'revolver',
'bazooka', 'machine gun']
mg1 = "I am going to use " + guns[2].title()
+ " in my next battle."
print(mg1)

I am going to use Revolver in my next
battle.
```

You can also use multiple values in the same sentence by the following method.

```
guns = ['shotgun', 'pistol', 'revolver',
'bazooka', 'machine gun']
mg1 = "I am going to use " + guns[2].title()
+ " in my next battle."
print(mg1)
mg1 = "I am going to use " + guns[4].title()
+ " in my next battle."
print(mg1)
mg1 = "I am going to use " + guns[0].title()
+ " in my next battle."
print(mg1)

I am going to use Revolver in my next
battle.
I am going to use Machine Gun in my next
battle.
I am going to use Shotgun in my next battle.
```

List Modification

Most lists are dynamic lists, so you can build a list and then add or remove different elements from the same as your program runs. For example, if a player is in the game, he is using guns to fight battles. You can store the initial number and type of guns in a list. Once the player empties the guns, you can remove them from the list. Each time the player finds a new gun off a dead soldier, you can add the same to the list. The list of your guns will keep decreasing and increasing throughout the game. Similarly, you can create other games that need addition and removal to lists constantly.

You can modify a list element in the same way you can access elements from a list. If you seek to change an element, you need to use the name of the list and the index number of the item that should be changed. After that, you should fill in the new value that you want that item to have.

I will use the list of guns that I have created earlier on and modify different items in the list.

```
guns = ['shotgun', 'pistol', 'revolver',
'bazooka', 'machine gun']
print(guns)

guns[0] = 'Ak-47'
print(guns)

guns[2] = 'knife'
print(guns)

['shotgun', 'pistol', 'revolver', 'bazooka',
'machine gun']
```

```
['Ak-47', 'pistol', 'revolver', 'bazooka',
'machine gun']
['Ak-47', 'pistol', 'knife', 'bazooka',
'machine gun']
```

I defined the list at the first line of code. Then I changed the values at index 0 and index 2, displaying the modified output accordingly. That's how you can change the output of any item in the list.

Adding elements to Python lists is also quite easy. You might need to add new elements to a specific list for different reasons. As I have explained earlier, if you are developing a game with a player who fights a battle, you need to know how to add elements to allow the player to pick up or buy different guns.

Append

The simplest form of addition of elements to lists in Python is through the append method. When you try to append an item to a Python list, the new element is immediately added to the tail of the list. I will use the same list and try to add new elements to it through the append method.

```
guns = ['shotgun', 'pistol', 'revolver',
'bazooka', 'machine gun']
print(guns)

guns.append('Ak-47')
print(guns)

guns.append('sten gun')
print(guns)
```

```
['shotgun', 'pistol', 'revolver', 'bazooka',
'machine gun']
['shotgun', 'pistol', 'revolver', 'bazooka',
'machine gun', 'Ak-47']
['shotgun', 'pistol', 'revolver', 'bazooka',
'machine gun', 'Ak-47', 'sten gun']
```

What is remarkable about the append method is that it adds different items to the end of the list without producing any changes in the order of the elements in the list. This makes the append method the most favorite method to build lists dynamically. You can take an empty list and add items to it gradually. This will take a series of append statements. In the following example, I will create an empty list and add elements to the same through the append() method.

```
guns = []
guns.append('Ak-47')
guns.append('sten gun')
guns.append('shotgun')
guns.append('pistol')
guns.append('revolver')
guns.append('bazooka')
guns.append('machine gun')
print(guns)

['Ak-47', 'sten gun', 'shotgun', 'pistol',
'revolver', 'bazooka', 'machine gun']
```

Building lists by this method is quite common because you will never know what data your users need to store in a specific program until after the start of the program. By the append() method, you can put your users in complete control. Just start by defining the list that is going to hold the values of users. After that, they can go on and fill up the list.

Another method to perform addition is the insert() method. You can add as many new items to the list through the insert() method as you need. All you need is to specify the index number of the new element and then the value of the new item.

```
guns = ['shotgun', 'pistol', 'revolver',
'bazooka', 'machine gun']
print(guns)
guns.insert(0, 'Ak-47')
print(guns)
guns.insert(2, 'sten gun')
print(guns)

['shotgun', 'pistol', 'revolver', 'bazooka',
'machine gun']
['Ak-47', 'shotgun', 'pistol', 'revolver',
'bazooka', 'machine gun']
['Ak-47', 'shotgun', 'sten gun', 'pistol',
'revolver', 'bazooka', 'machine gun']
```

You can see that I added different items at the locations I wanted to by using the insert() method. The insert() method pops open space at positions 0 and 2 to add elements that I proposed. This operation shifts the position of other values in the list to the right of the list.

Removing Elements

You also can remove elements from the list. For example, when your player empties a gun and wants to get rid of it, you need to have a method that removes that item from the list.

If you know exactly what position the item holds in the list, you can use the del statement and use the index number to slice out the element from the list. This helps create a dynamic game where the player can see the list and throw away a specific gun from his list of guns.

```
guns = ['shotgun', 'pistol', 'revolver',
'bazooka', 'machine gun']
print(guns)

del guns[0]
print(guns)

del guns[2]
print(guns)

['shotgun', 'pistol', 'revolver', 'bazooka',
'machine gun']
['pistol', 'revolver', 'bazooka', 'machine
gun']
['pistol', 'revolver', 'machine gun']
```

You can see that you can remove items from any positions in the list. However, what is remarkable about the del() method is that you can no longer access the deleted values in any way.

Another method to remove elements from the list is the pop() method. You might want to use the elements once you have removed them from the list in a game. For example, you may want to allow the players to see the list of guns that have been emptied and thrown away. At this point, you need to use the pop() method to achieve the objective that you want to.

The pop() method removes items from the end of the list. It also lets you work with popped-out items. The term pop is derived from the idea of comparing lists with stacks of different items and popping those items off the top. In this analogy, the top of the stack is akin to the end of the list.

```
guns = ['shotgun', 'pistol', 'revolver',
'bazooka', 'machine gun']
print(guns)

popped_guns = guns.pop()
print(guns)
print(popped_guns)

popped_guns = guns.pop()
print(guns)
print(popped_guns)

popped_guns = guns.pop()
print(guns)
print(popped_guns)

['shotgun', 'pistol', 'revolver', 'bazooka',
'machine gun']
['shotgun', 'pistol', 'revolver', 'bazooka']
machine gun
['shotgun', 'pistol', 'revolver']
bazooka
['shotgun', 'pistol']
revolver
```

You can see that not only was I able to delete items from the list, but I was also able to use the deleted items to display them in the interpreter.

I defined the list and printed the items in the list. Then I popped one value and stored it in the variable popped_guns. Then I printed the revised list to show that the item is no longer on the list. After that, I printed the popped value to prove that I could still access it. I repeated the removal three times, and it worked perfectly.

Let us see how you can use the pop method in the game you have been developing to remove values. In the following example, I will show how you can use the value of the removed item. In the example, I will use the popped value in a statement to display a message to the player.

```
guns = ['shotgun', 'pistol', 'revolver',
'bazooka', 'machine gun']

popped_guns = guns.pop()
print("The last emptied gun was a " +
popped_guns.title() + ".")

popped_guns = guns.pop()
print("The last emptied gun was a " +
popped_guns.title() + ".")

popped_guns = guns.pop()
print("The last emptied gun was a " +
popped_guns.title() + ".")

The last emptied gun was a Machine Gun.
The last emptied gun was a Bazooka.
The last emptied gun was a Revolver.
```

The output comes in the form of a simple sentence about the recent gun that the player owns.

You also can mention the index number from a designated position in the list. You can use the pop() method to remove different items from any positions in a list. See how it is done.

```
guns = ['shotgun', 'pistol', 'revolver',
'bazooka', 'machine gun']

popped_guns = guns.pop(0)
print("The " + popped_guns.title() + " is
emptied and thrown away.")

popped_guns = guns.pop(2)
print("The " + popped_guns.title() + " is
emptied and thrown away.")

The Shotgun is emptied and thrown away.
The Bazooka is emptied and thrown away.
```

I popped an item from the list and then used it to print a message that told the player about the gun that was emptied and thrown away. Each time you use the pop() method, the item you have been working with will no longer be stored inside the list.

If you cannot decide whether you have to use the pop() method or the del statement, you can decide based on the fact if you have to use the item later on or not.

Remove() Method

You may not know the exact position of a value at a point, which is why you have to use the value itself to remove it from the list. If you have got all the values in the list, you can use the remove()

method. I will use values to delete different items from the list in the following example.

```
guns = ['shotgun', 'pistol', 'revolver',
'bazooka', 'machine gun']
print(guns)

guns.remove('revolver')
print(guns)

guns.remove('shotgun')
print(guns)

['shotgun', 'pistol', 'revolver', 'bazooka',
'machine gun']
['shotgun', 'pistol', 'bazooka', 'machine
gun']
['pistol', 'bazooka', 'machine gun']
```

This method is considered one of the most efficient methods to remove items from a list. You can also use the remove() method to operate on a value removed from the list. I will take the removed value and use it in a list.

```
guns = ['shotgun', 'pistol', 'revolver',
'bazooka', 'machine gun']
print(guns)

emptied_gun = 'pistol'
guns.remove(emptied_gun)
print(guns)
print("\nThe " + emptied_gun.title() + " is
empty and is being thrown away.")

emptied_gun = 'bazooka'
```

```
guns.remove(emptied_gun)
print(guns)
print("\nThe " + emptied_gun.title() + " is
empty and is being thrown away.")

['shotgun', 'pistol', 'revolver', 'bazooka',
'machine gun']
['shotgun', 'revolver', 'bazooka', 'machine
gun']

The Pistol is empty and is being thrown
away.
['shotgun', 'revolver', 'machine gun']

The Bazooka is empty and is being thrown
away.
```

After I had defined the list, I stored the value inside a variable, namely emptied_gun. Then I used the same value to instruct Python on how it should be used in a print statement. The remove() method only deletes the first occurrence of the value that you have specified.

List Organization

Your lists, more often, will be created in a highly unpredictable order because you cannot control the order in which the users will enter data on the website. Although this may appear to be unavoidable in many circumstances, you may need to present the information in perfect order. Sometimes you may need to preserve the original order in which the list was first developed. At other times, you may need to change the order. Python provides multiple ways for organizing lists.

Permanent Method

The sort() method in Python makes it easy to sort out the list. I will use the same to explain how to use the sort() method. I am assuming that the values that are stored in the list are in lowercase.

```
guns = ['shotgun', 'pistol', 'revolver',
'bazooka', 'machine gun']
guns.sort()
print(guns)

['bazooka', 'machine gun', 'pistol',
'revolver', 'shotgun']
```

The order will come out in alphabetical order. The order has permanently changed. You cannot revert it to the original order. You also can sort the list in the reverse alphabetical order by passing the argument reverse=True to sort() method. In the following example, I will sort the lists in reverse alphabetical order.

Sorted() Function

To maintain the original order of the list but still keep it sorted, you may use the sorted() function. The sorted() function will let you display the list in a specific order, but it will not affect the original order.

```
fruits = ['orange', 'dragon fruit',
'jackfruit', 'strawberry', 'apple']
print("This is the original order:")
print(fruits)

print("\nThis list is sorted by the sorted()
function.")
```

```
print(sorted(fruits))

print("\nThis again is the original list.")
print(fruits)

This is the original order:
['orange', 'dragon fruit', 'jackfruit',
'strawberry', 'apple']

This list is sorted by the sorted()
function.
['apple', 'dragon fruit', 'jackfruit',
'orange', 'strawberry']

This again is the original list.
['orange', 'dragon fruit', 'jackfruit',
'strawberry', 'apple']
```

You can see that the list retains the original order. The sorted() function also accepts the reverse=True argument if you are looking to display a list that is in the reverse alphabetical order.

Sorting a list in alphabetical order is a complicated job if the values are not in lowercase. There are many ways to interpret capital letters when you have to sort the order of the list.

Reverse Order

If you want to reverse the order of a list, you have to use the reverse() method. It will reverse the chronological order of the list. It does not reorder the list in alphabetical order. It simply reverses the original order of the list. This change, too, is permanent and cannot be restored. But you can revert the order of the list by using the reverse() method the second time on the changed list.

```
fruits = ['orange', 'dragon fruit',
'jackfruit', 'strawberry', 'apple']
print(fruits)

fruits.reverse()
print(fruits)

['orange', 'dragon fruit', 'jackfruit',
'strawberry', 'apple']
['apple', 'strawberry', 'jackfruit', 'dragon
fruit', 'orange']
```

If I apply the same reverse method to the changed list, I will have the originally ordered list back.

```
fruits = ['orange', 'dragon fruit',
'jackfruit', 'strawberry', 'apple']
print(fruits)

fruits.reverse()
print(fruits)

fruits.reverse()
print(fruits)

['orange', 'dragon fruit', 'jackfruit',
'strawberry', 'apple']
['apple', 'strawberry', 'jackfruit', 'dragon
fruit', 'orange']
['orange', 'dragon fruit', 'jackfruit',
'strawberry', 'apple']
```

List Length

There is a dedicated function to find out the length of the list. The function is named as the len() function. See how it works.

```
>>> fruits = ['orange', 'dragon fruit',
'jackfruit', 'strawberry', 'apple']
>>> len(fruits)
5
```

This function is useful when identifying the total number of fruits or guns in the list. For example, in your game, if the player wants to know how many guns he has to play with, he can use the function to display the total number on the screen. This simple function will add more charm to your game or application. If you are building a grocery app, you can let the user count the number of fruits that he has added to the cart by this function.

Looping Through Lists

You may often need to run through the list entries while performing the same tasks with each item. For example, if you are building a game, you may need to move every element on your screen in a list of numbers, and you may need to perform the statistical operation on each element.

If you are developing a battle-oriented game, you may allow the user to display the list of guns on the screen to know what kind of guns he has before he jumps into the battle. This will also allow him to formulate an attack strategy for which gun is suitable to which point of the battle. A simple loop can help you make your game and application more dynamic and user-friendly. Python loops with lists are also used when you have to perform the same action with all the items in the list.

Let us say that we have a complete list of fruits, and we want to use all the items in the list. I can do this by retrieving all the names of the fruits from the list individually. However, this approach may cause several problems. Instead of writing separate codes for each item, I will use a loop to perform the same action repeatedly. A for loop avoids repetition in writing codes to perform an action on lists. I will now use the for loop to print all the names in the list.

```
fruits = ['orange', 'dragon fruit',
'jackfruit', 'strawberry', 'apple']
for fruit in fruits:
    print(fruit)

orange
dragon fruit
jackfruit
strawberry
apple
```

I defined the list in the first step, and then I created the for loop that would iterate through each item in the list and display it neatly in the output. The concept of looping in the world of Python is important because it is the most common way to execute repetitive tasks. The first line that contains the for keyword tells Python to retrieve the first value in the list and then store it onwards into the variable, namely fruit. Then it reads the next line and prints the name of the value. After it prints the first value, it returns to the first line that has the for keyword because it finds out that the list has more values left on which it has to work.

You should keep in mind that the set of steps are repeated for each item of the list, no matter how many items exist in the list. If the list has a million items, Python will repeat all the steps a million times. Also, the speed of the execution of tasks is important. You can do many things in the loop. I will use the same list of fruits and print a message through the for loop.

```
fruits = ['orange', 'dragon fruit', 
'jackfruit', 'strawberry', 'apple']
for fruit in fruits:
    print("The " + fruit.title() + " is ripe for the taking.")

The Orange is ripe for the taking.
The Dragon Fruit is ripe for the taking.
The Jackfruit is ripe for the taking.
The Strawberry is ripe for the taking.
The Apple is ripe for the taking.
```

In this code, I have added a message that included all items from the list. The first item to loop through is the value of the fruit Orange. The second is Dragon Fruit, and the last to display is Apple. I have added only five items to the list. You can add more items to test the ability of the loop and lists. In the output, you can see a personalized message.

You can write as many codes as you like in the for loop. In the next example, I will add two more lines of code to the same sample. These will be the second and third lines of code to display a broader message.

```
fruits = ['dragon fruit', 'jackfruit',
'strawberry']
for fruit in fruits:
    print("The " + fruit.title() + " is ripe
for the taking.")
    print("I will start picking " +
fruit.title() + " next Monday.")
    print("The packing of " + fruit.title()
+ " for export will start next month.")

The Dragon Fruit is ripe for the taking.
I will start picking Dragon Fruit next
Monday.
The packing of Dragon Fruit for export will
start next month.
The Jackfruit is ripe for the taking.
I will start picking Jackfruit next Monday.
The packing of Jackfruit for export will
start next month.
The Strawberry is ripe for the taking.
I will start picking Strawberry next Monday.
The packing of Strawberry for export will
start next month.
```

As each print statement is indented, each code line must be executed once for all the fruits in the list. However, there still is one problem. There is no black line in between the lines of code. This is not neat and needs to change.

```
fruits = ['dragon fruit', 'jackfruit',
'strawberry']
for fruit in fruits:
    print("The " + fruit.title() + " is ripe
for the taking.")
```

```
    print("I will start picking " +
fruit.title() + " next Monday.")
    print("The packing of " + fruit.title()
+ " for export will start next month.\n")

The Dragon Fruit is ripe for the taking.
I will start picking Dragon Fruit next
Monday.
The packing of Dragon Fruit for export will
start next month.

The Jackfruit is ripe for the taking.
I will start picking Jackfruit next Monday.
The packing of Jackfruit for export will
start next month.

The Strawberry is ripe for the taking.
I will start picking Strawberry next Monday.
The packing of Strawberry for export will
start next month.
```

Once the loop has ended, you can end it creatively by displaying a neat message to the users. You may want to summarize what has happened in the loop. You can easily summarize the block of output or shift to the other work that the program needs to accomplish.

```
The lines of code that come after the for
loop that are no longer indented will be
executed without any repetition. This makes
indentation highly important. It can produce
serious errors if you don't do it right.
fruits = ['dragon fruit', 'jackfruit',
'strawberry']
for fruit in fruits:
```

```
    print("The " + fruit.title() + " is ripe
for the taking.")
    print("I will start picking " +
fruit.title() + " next Monday.")
    print("The packing of " + fruit.title()
+ " for export will start next month.\n")

print("All the fruits need to be double-
checked before export.")

The Dragon Fruit is ripe for the taking.
I will start picking Dragon Fruit next
Monday.
The packing of Dragon Fruit for export will
start next month.

The Jackfruit is ripe for the taking.
I will start picking Jackfruit next Monday.
The packing of Jackfruit for export will
start next month.

The Strawberry is ripe for the taking.
I will start picking Strawberry next Monday.
The packing of Strawberry for export will
start next month.

All the fruits need to be double-checked
before export.
```

When you process data by using the for loop, you will find out that this is the best way to summarize a specific operation usually performed on a complete data set. For an app that deals with groceries, you can let the users go through all the fruits and vegetable items to see what is available to buy.

Indentation

Python is strict about indentation. It uses indentation to sense the connection between different lines of code. In the above-mentioned examples, the lines that printed messages about different fruits became part of the loop because of their indentation. Python's indentation makes code smoother to read. It basically uses whitespace to compel you to write code in a neatly formatted way with a clear structure. In lengthy Python programs, you may notice certain blocks of code that are indented at various levels.

Once you realize how to keep up proper indentation in your code, you will make fewer indentation errors. Sometimes, people indent blocks of code that are not supposed to be indented. Once you see these errors, you will immediately realize how to fix them.

```
>>> fruits = ['dragon fruit', 'jackfruit', 'strawberry']
>>> for fruit in fruits:
print("The " + fruit.title() + " is ripe for the taking.")
SyntaxError: expected an indented block
Just indent the last line of code to fix this error.
```

You may have indented the first line of code after the for statement, but you forgot to indent the subsequent lines. This kind of error is possible when you try to execute multiple tasks at the same time. Here is the result of a forgotten indentation for the second and third lines.

```
fruits = ['dragon fruit', 'jackfruit',
'strawberry']
for fruit in fruits:
    print("The " + fruit.title() + " is ripe
for the taking.")
print("I will start picking " +
fruit.title() + " next Monday.")
print("The packing of " + fruit.title() + "
for export will start next month.\n")

The Dragon Fruit is ripe for the taking.
The Jackfruit is ripe for the taking.
The Strawberry is ripe for the taking.
I will start picking Strawberry next Monday.
The packing of Strawberry for export will
start next month.
```

The loop did not work on the second and third print statements. It only worked on the first value in the item and left out the result of them. So, those that are not indented will be automatically left out of the iterations of the loop. This is called a logical error. The syntax is a valid Python code and what is left in the code is logic. If you find out in your code that a certain action should have been repeated, but it is not, you need to determine whether there are some lines of code that should be simply indented or not.

Unnecessary Indentation

If you add an unnecessary indent, it will also produce an error.

```
>>> fruits = ['dragon fruit']
>>>    print(fruits)

SyntaxError: unexpected indent
```

Post-Loop Unnecessary Indentation

If you have accidentally indented a code that you have written as a finisher after the loop, the code will also be repeated just like other codes do. It will be repeated for each item in the list. Sometimes, this will prompt Python to produce an error, but you will often see a logical error. Let us see how it behaves in Python 3.8.

```
fruits = ['dragon fruit', 'jackfruit', 'strawberry']
for fruit in fruits:
    print("The " + fruit.title() + " is ripe for the taking.")
    print("I will start picking " + fruit.title() + " next Monday.")
    print("The packing of " + fruit.title() + " for export will start next month.\n")

    print("All the fruits need to be double-checked before export.")
```

The Dragon Fruit is ripe for the taking.
I will start picking Dragon Fruit next Monday.
The packing of Dragon Fruit for export will start next month.

All the fruits need to be double-checked before export.
The Jackfruit is ripe for the taking.
I will start picking Jackfruit next Monday.
The packing of Jackfruit for export will start next month.

```
All the fruits need to be double-checked
before export.
The Strawberry is ripe for the taking.
I will start picking Strawberry next Monday.
The packing of Strawberry for export will
start next month.

All the fruits need to be double-checked
before export.
```

Instead of producing an error, Python 3.8 has repeated the statement for all the items in the list. This is known as the logical error. Python does not know what to do with a wrongful indentation in the code. It runs all the written code in the form of valid syntax. If the action is repeated several times when it needs to be executed once, look out for whether you need to unindent a portion of the code that is being unnecessarily repeated.

Numerical Lists

There are several reasons for storing different sets of numbers. You may need to keep track of the enemies in a battle game. You may need to point out the number of targets in the game. Lists are perfect for storing numbers, and Python offers a set of tools to help you work efficiently with numerical lists. Once you have understood how to use the tools correctly, your code will work perfectly when the lists you are working on contains millions of items.

The range() Function

The first function for a numerical list is the range() function, which makes it easy to generate different series of numbers. You can use this range() function for printing different series of numbers such as the following:

```
for num in range(1,7):
    print(num)
```

1
2
3
4
5
6

You can see that the range() function prints only numbers from 1 to 6. This is due to its off-by-one style that you will more often see in many programming languages. The range() function causes Python to initiate counting at the very first value. It stops when it finally reaches the second value that you provide to it. Because it seizes at the second value, the output will never contain the last value. If you want to include the digit 7 in the output, you need to extend the range to 8.

```
for num in range(1,8):
    print(num)
```

1
2
3
4
5

6
7

You can use the range() function to create a list of numbers. You can convert the result of the range() function directly into the list() function. When you wrap up list() around the range() function, the output is a list of numbers. In the next example, I will shift the result of the range() function into a list.

```
num = list(range(1,8))
print(num)
```

[1, 2, 3, 4, 5, 6, 7]

You also can use the range() function to tell Python what numbers to skip and what to include. See the demonstration in the following example.

```
even_num = list(range(4, 22, 4))
print(even_num)
```

[4, 8, 12, 16, 20]

You can use the range() function to produce the square of each integer from 1 to 22. Two asterisks ** in Python represent exponents. Here is how you can do that.

```
square_num = []
for num in range(1, 22):
    square = num**2
    square_num.append(square)

print(square_num)
```

```
[1, 4, 9, 16, 25, 36, 49, 64, 81, 100, 121,
144, 169, 196, 225, 256, 289, 324, 361, 400,
441]
```

I started the code with an empty list known as square_num. Then I told Python to initiate a loop through each value between 1 and 22 using the range function. The present value is raised to the second power in the loop and stored inside the variable square. When the loop completes its run, the list of squares comes out as printed.

List Slicing

You can produce slices of a list and use them at will. To create a slice of a list, you need to specify the index of the starting and ending elements in the list. Like the range() function, Python will stop one item short of the second index. If you need to include three elements, you have to set the index at 0 and 3. See how it works.

```
fruits = ['orange', 'dragon fruit',
'jackfruit', 'strawberry', 'apple']
print(fruits[0:3])

['orange', 'dragon fruit', 'jackfruit']
```

You can generate different subsets of the list.

```
fruits = ['orange', 'dragon fruit',
'jackfruit', 'strawberry', 'apple']
print(fruits[1:3])

['dragon fruit', 'jackfruit']
```

If you omit the first index number, Python will consider it to be the start of the list.

```
fruits = ['orange', 'dragon fruit',
'jackfruit', 'strawberry', 'apple']
print(fruits[:4])

['orange', 'dragon fruit', 'jackfruit',
'strawberry']
```

You can see that Python started the sliced list from the start. If you leave out the last index, it will run its course to the end of the list.

```
fruits = ['orange', 'dragon fruit',
'jackfruit', 'strawberry', 'apple']
print(fruits[1:])

['dragon fruit', 'jackfruit', 'strawberry',
'apple']
```

You can also use negative indexing to slice the lists.

```
fruits = ['orange', 'dragon fruit',
'jackfruit', 'strawberry', 'apple']
print(fruits[-4:])

['dragon fruit', 'jackfruit', 'strawberry',
'apple']
```

Looping Through Slices

You can use integrate the for loop in the code to create a loop through the slice that you produce.

```
fruits = ['dragon fruit', 'jackfruit',
'strawberry', 'banana', 'peach', 'guava']
for fruit in fruits[:5]:
    print("The " + fruit.title() + " is ripe
for the taking.")
```

```
    print("I will start picking " +
fruit.title() + " next Monday.")
```

```
The Dragon Fruit is ripe for the taking.
I will start picking Dragon Fruit next
Monday.
The Jackfruit is ripe for the taking.
I will start picking Jackfruit next Monday.
The Strawberry is ripe for the taking.
I will start picking Strawberry next Monday.
The Banana is ripe for the taking.
I will start picking Banana next Monday.
The Peach is ripe for the taking.
I will start picking Peach next Monday.
```

Instead of looping through the entire list, Python will only loop through the elements present in the slice. Slicing can be highly useful in several situations. For example, when you have to create a game, you can add a player's final score to the list when a player finishes playing.

Copying Lists

You may often want to start the existing list and then create a completely new list based on the original one. Let us see how the copying function in a list works and then examine the situation in which copying the list remains useful. If you want to copy a list, create a slice that will include the original list. You have to omit the first and the last indexes like this ([:]). This will tell Python to create a slice that will start with the first item and ends with the last. Here is a list of books.

```
books = ['great expectations', 'god of
flies', 'tempest', 'middle march', 'bleak
house', 'hard times']
favorite_books = books[:]

print("These are the books I have in my
library:")
print(books)

print("These are my favorite books:")
print(favorite_books)
```

These are the books I have in my library:

```
['great expectations', 'god of flies',
'tempest', 'middle march', 'bleak house',
'hard times']
```

These are my favorite books:

```
['great expectations', 'god of flies',
'tempest', 'middle march', 'bleak house',
'hard times']
```

So, we have a perfect copy of the list that we created at the start. If you are still in doubt whether they are two separate lists or not, you can add a new book to each list.

```
books = ['great expectations', 'god of
flies', 'tempest', 'middle march', 'bleak
house', 'hard times']
favorite_books = books[:]

books.append('othello')
favorite_books.append('heart of darkness')
```

```
print("These are the books I have in my
library:")
print(books)

print("These are my favorite books:")
print(favorite_books)
```

These are the books I have in my library:

```
['great expectations', 'god of flies',
'tempest', 'middle march', 'bleak house',
'hard times', 'othello']
```

These are my favorite books:

```
['great expectations', 'god of flies',
'tempest', 'middle march', 'bleak house',
'hard times', 'heart of darkness']
```

First, I copied the original list into a new list and then added new items to each list. If you copy a list without a slice, here is what happens.

```
books = ['great expectations', 'god of
flies', 'bleak house', 'hard times']
favorite_books = books

books.append('othello')
favorite_books.append('heart of darkness')

print("These are the books I have in my
library:")
print(books)

print("\nThese are my favorite books:")
print(favorite_books)
```

These are the books I have in my library:

```
['great expectations', 'god of flies',
'bleak house', 'hard times', 'othello',
'heart of darkness']
```

These are my favorite books:

```
['great expectations', 'god of flies',
'bleak house', 'hard times', 'othello',
'heart of darkness']
```

You can see that both items have been added to both lists. They behaved not like two but like one list.

Chapter Four

Python Tuples

Lists are useful to store different sets of items that change throughout a program. Their tendency to modify is highly important, especially when working with a certain list of users on a particular website or different characters inside a game. However, sometimes you may feel the desire to create a list that must not be changed. Tuples allow programmers to do exactly that. Python refers to different values that cannot be changed as immutable values. An immutable list is named a tuple.

> A tuple looks exactly like a list except that it has square brackets instead of parentheses to enclose the items. Once you have defined a tuple, you can access the elements inside it, but you cannot modify them in any sense. Python tuples are one of the four built-in data types in Python. The other three are lists, sets, and dictionaries, and all of these data types have different qualities and usage capacities. Tuples are enclosed inside round brackets. Here is how a tuple is created and how it looks like.

```
mytuple = ("cars, bikes, motorbikes, buses,
tanks, ships")
print(mytuple)

cars, bikes, motorbikes, buses, tanks, ships
```

The items in a tuple are in an ordered form. They are unchangeable, and they also allow duplicate values. The items in the tuple are indexed. The first item is indexed as [0]. This is how the number goes on.

When you say that tuples are in ordered form, this alludes to the fact that all the items inside a tuple fall into a defined order. That order does not change. You can add or remove any items from a tuple once you have created them.

Since tuples come in indexed form, you can add duplicate values inside a tuple. See the following example.

```
mytuple = ("cars, bikes, motorbikes, buses,
tanks, ships, bikes")
print(mytuple)

cars, bikes, motorbikes, buses, tanks,
ships, bikes
```

Length

You can calculate the length of a tuple by the following function.

```
mytuple = ("cars, bikes, motorbikes, buses,
tanks, ships, bikes")
print(len(mytuple))
51
```

If you want to create a tuple with just one item, you need to add a comma after that one item. Otherwise, Python will never recognize it as a tuple.

This is how the result looks like if you don't add a comma after the first item in the tuple.

```
mytuple = ("cars")
print(mytuple)

cars
```

Here is how the result will look like after you add a comma to the code.

```
mytuple = ("cars",)
print(mytuple)

('cars',)
```

Changing Elements

Let us see what happens when you try to change an item in the tuple.

```
mytuple = ("cars, bikes, motorbikes, buses, tanks, ships, bikes")
mytuple[0] = "jets"
```

Traceback (most recent call last):

```
    File "C:/Users/saifia computers/Desktop/python.py", line 2, in <module>
        mytuple[0] = "jets"
```

TypeError: 'str' object does not support item assignment

When the code tries to change the value of the item at the first index, Python returns a type error. As you are trying to change a tuple, you cannot do that. That's why you run an error. Python tells you that you cannot assign a new value to the item in the tuple.

Creating Loop

You can build and run a loop through a tuple just like you did with lists. Let us see how to write the code for building a loop and running it through the tuple.

```
mytuples = ("cars", "bikes", "motorbikes",
"buses", "tanks", "ships", "bikes")
for mytuple in mytuples:
    print(mytuple)

cars
bikes
motorbikes
buses
tanks
ships
bikes
```

Overwriting a Tuple

You cannot modify the tuple, but you can overwrite it by assigning it new values. You can assign new values to the variables that carry a tuple. Therefore, if you need to change the values of a tuple, you can simply redefine the entire tuple.

```
mytuples = ("cars", "bikes", "motorbikes",
"buses", "tanks", "ships", "bikes")
print("This is the original tuple:")
for mytuple in mytuples:
    print(mytuple)

mytuples = ("jets", "bikes", "motorbikes",
"buses", "tanks", "ships", "bikes")
print("\nThis is the modified tuple:")
for mytuple in mytuples:
    print(mytuple)
```

This is the original tuple:

```
cars
bikes
motorbikes
buses
tanks
ships
bikes
```

This is the modified tuple:

```
jets
bikes
motorbikes
buses
tanks
ships
bikes
```

The code defines the original tuple, prints the initial values, and then stores the new tuple inside the modified values. Python does not return any error because it allows overwriting a tuple.

If you compare tuples with lists, you will understand that these are simple data structures. You can use them when you have to store different sets of values that need not be changed throughout a program's life.

Code Styling

When you are writing a long program, you should know how to style your code. You need to take the time to make sure that your code is easy to read and understand. Writing easily comprehensible code can help you track down what your programs do, and it also helps you understand the code.

Python programmers have largely agreed upon different styling traditions to ensure that every person's code is properly structured in the same manner. Once you have learned to write a neat and clean code, you will understand the structure of other's code as well. If you hope to become a professional programmer at any point in your life, you need to begin following the guidelines as soon as possible.

If someone tries to change the Python language, they start writing Python Enhancement Proposal (PEP). One of the oldest PEPs is the PEP8. It instructs Python programmers on how they can style their code. PEP 8 is fairly lengthy. However, most can relate to a highly complex coding structure than what you might have seen until now.

The Python style guide was produced with the aim that code is easily read than it is written. You will write your code once and start reading it as you begin the process of debugging. When you add new features to a Python program, you will need to spend time reading the code. When you share your code with other programmers, they will be able to read the code easily.

Between the choice of writing code that is easier to read or write, Python programmers encourage you to write code that can be easily readable by others.

PEP8 recommends that you should use four spaces for each indentation level. Using four spaces will improve the readability while leaving the room for multiple indentation levels on each line of code. In a word processing document, you might have used tabs instead of spaces. This works well because it makes the paragraphs easily readable. The Python interpreter does not easily distinguish between tabs and spaces. It looks at each differently. Every text editor has a setting that provides you the opportunity to use the TAB key. You should use the TAB key, making sure that the editor is all set to insert several spaces rather than the tabs in the document.

Most senior and professional programmers recommend that each line in Python code should not exceed 80 characters. This guideline has historically developed because most computers could fit only 79 characters on a single line inside a terminal window. Presently, people can fit longer lines on the screens, but other reasons exist to adhere to 79 characters. As professional programmers have several files opened on the screen, using the standard length of lines helps them see complete lines in two to three files that can be opened on side-by-side screens. PEP8 also recommends that you should limit the comments to 72 characters per line as some of the tools that would generate automatic documentation for bigger projects would add the formatting characters at the start of commented lines.

However, these guidelines are not final. You can change the character limit at will. You need not worry about the length of the line. Most editors allow you to view the lines in a vertical format on the screen. It will help you know the limit as well.

You can use blank lines to group different parts of the program in a visual format. You need to see blank lines for organizing the files, but you should not do so excessively. Blank lines do not affect how your code runs. The Python interpreter uses horizontal indentation for interpreting the deep meaning in the code. However, it utterly disregards any kind of vertical spacing.

Chapter Five

Python Conditionals

Programming involves the examination of different conditions and making decisions based on those conditions. The Python if statement will allow you to examine the present state of a Python program and also respond to the same most appropriately to the same state.

This chapter will walk you through different conditional tests that allow you to test any condition. You will learn how to write the if statements, and you will also learn how to build a complex series of conditional statements when you can sense that the exact conditions are present. After that, you will be able to apply the concept to lists.

I will start with a short example that shows how if tests can allow you to respond to special situations properly. Just take a list of different types of bike companies and print the name of each of them. The names are proper names, and they should be printed in the title case. Some of them also need to be printed in upper case as well. See how the code works.

```
bikes = ("toyota", "bmw", "suzuki",
"yamaha", "harley davidson", "honda")
for bike in bikes:
    if bike == 'bmw':
        print(bike.upper())
    else:
        print(bike.title())

Toyota
BMW
Suzuki
Yamaha
Harley Davidson
Honda
```

The for loop in this example will check if the current value of the bike is bmw. If it finds it true, the value will be neatly printed in uppercase. If the value of the bike is not bmw and something else, it will print it in the title case.

In this example, I have combined several concepts that you will learn in the incoming sections. Let us start by looking at the types of tests that you may use to examine the program's conditions.

The core of if statements is the conditional test. This rests at the heart of the if statement. It is an expression that may be evaluated as False or True and is known as the conditional test. Python uses True and False values to decide whether the code in the if-statement needs to be executed or not. If the conditional test is true, Python will execute code that follows the if statement. If the test turns out to be false, Python will ignore the code and the if statement.

Most conditional tests tend to compare the values of a specific variable to the value of interest. The simplest of the conditional tests will check if the variable's value is equal to the value of interest.

```
>>> bike = 'bmw'
>>> bike == 'bmw'
True
>>>
```

At the first line of the code, the value of the bike is set at 'bmw.' I used the single equal sign in the code to. The second line of code tests if the value of the bike is bmw by using the double equal signs. This is known as the equality operator. It will return True if the values to the right and left sides of the operator match. It will return False if the values to the right and left do not match. As the values to the right and left sides match in this code, the result is True. Let us see another example.

```
>>> bike = 'bmw'
>>> bike == 'honda'
False
>>>
```

When you check for equality and ignore the value's case, you will see a different result than you had expected. Testing for equality is extremely case-sensitive in the world of Python. For example, two values that have different capitalization will never be considered equal.

```
>>> bike = 'bmw'
>>> bike == 'Bmw'
```

```
False
>>>
```

If case is important, the behavior is advantageous. When it does not matter, and you need to test the value of a variable, you may be able to convert the value of a variable into lowercase before running the comparison.

```
>>> bike = 'BMW'
>>> bike.lower() == 'bmw'
True
>>>
```

Different websites enforce a set of rules for the data that the users will enter in a similar manner. For example, a website may use a conditional test like this to ensure that each user carries a unique username and not simply a variation on the capitalization of that person's username. When a person submits their username, the new username is immediately converted into lowercase and then compared to the lowercase versions of usernames. The username Adam will be immediately rejected if the system is already using any variation of 'adam.'

If you want to determine if the two values are equal or not, you may combine an equal sign with an exclamation point. The exclamation denotes a 'not' as it does in most of the programming languages. Now I will use another if statement to test how we can use the inequality operator.

```
ordered_dessert = ('chocolate cake')
if ordered_dessert != 'fruit salad':
    print("Please serve the fruit salad.")
```

```
Please serve the fruit salad.
```

On the first line, I compared the values of ordered_dessert to fruit salad. If the values don't match, Python declares it true and executes the code. If the values match, Python returns False and stops running the code. As the value of ordered_dessert is not fruit salad, the code is immediately executed. Most conditional expressions that you write will test for equality. However, sometimes you will find it highly efficient if you test it for inequality.

Numerical Testing

You also can do numerical testing. See the following statements to learn how Python tests numbers and returns results.

```
the_answer = 45
if the_answer != 55:
    print("Your answer is incorrect. Please try to run the code again.")

Your answer is incorrect. Please try to run the code again.
```

The conditional test passes because the value 45 is not equal to 55. Because the test is meant to pass, the indented block of code is executed. Let us see what happens if the test does not pass.

```
the_answer = 45
if the_answer != 45:
    print("Your answer is incorrect. Please try to run the code again.")
```

83

If you run the code like this, you will see nothing on the interpreter screen.

Testing Multiple Conditions

You may need to check multiple conditions simultaneously. For example, you may need a couple of conditions to turn out to be true for taking action. Other times, you may be satisfied with one condition turning out to be true. The keywords *or* and *and* will aid you in these tricky situations.

If you want to check if two conditions are true, you need to use the *and* keyword to combine the conditional tests. If each test passes, the overall expression will be evaluated to be True. If either or both tests fail, the expression will be evaluated to be False.

For example, you may check if two persons are over 18 or not by using the following example.

```
>>> age1 = 25
>>> age2 = 18
>>> age1 >= 22 and age2 >= 17
True
Here is the second code.
>>> age1 = 25
>>> age2 = 18
>>> age1 >= 22 and age2 >= 20
False
```

You can also use *or* to check multiple conditions in Python. The *or* keyword will allow you to check different conditions, but it also passes when both or either of the individual tests will pass. The *or* expression will only fail when both tests fail. Let us use the *or* keyword in the following example.

```
>>> age1 = 22
>>> age2 = 18
>>> age1 >= 20 or age2 >= 20
True
>>> age1 = 18
>>> age1 >= 22 or age2 >= 21
False
>>>
```

The conditionals have some other important jobs to do as well. Sometimes you feel the need to check if a list contains a specific value before you take an action. For example, you might need to check if a certain bike vegetable exists in a list of vegetables. For example, if you develop a grocery app with a list of vegetables, you can use the conditionals to let users know if a certain vegetable exists in the list or not.

To find out if a specific value exists in a list, you have to use the word in. Let us consider a piece of code that you might use for a grocery app. I will create a list of vegetables from which a customer may select a vegetable to buy.

```
>>> veggies = ['potato', 'tomato', 'lettuce', 'cilantro', 'cabbage', 'pumpkin']
>>> 'tomato' in veggies
True
>>> 'pepper' in veggies
False
>>>
```

This method is extremely powerful because you can build a list of vegetables and then check if a certain value exists in the list while you match items.

Example

Sometimes it is important to know whether a specific value appears in a list or not. You can use the keyword, *not* in a specific situation. See how I use the vegetable list in a program.

```
veggies = ['potato', 'tomato', 'lettuce',
'cilantro', 'cabbage', 'pumpkin']
veg_item = 'pepper'
veg_item1 = 'bell pepper'

if veg_item not in veggies:
    print(veg_item.title() + " is not available at the store right now.")
    print(veg_item1.title() + " is not available at the store right now.")

Pepper is not available at the store right now.
Bell Pepper is not available at the store right now.
```

The first line of code tells Python to return True if the requisite value is not in the list. Then it goes on to execute the second line of code. The vegetables, pepper, and bell pepper are in the vegetables list, so Python displays the message neat and formatted.

The if Statement

When you get to know the conditional tests, you may start writing the *if* statements. There are different types of if statements in Python. Your choice of which you should use will depend on the total number of conditions that you are looking forward to testing. You have seen multiple examples of the *if* statements. Let us what the structure of each of them is and how they function.

Simple if

The simplest type of if statement has to perform one action. You can put this conditional test inside the first line and around any action in the indented block of code after the test. If the conditional test returns the True value, Python will execute the code that fails after the if statement. Let us say a variable represents the age of a person who seeks to join a golf club. To join the club, the person must be over the age of 18. The following lines of code will test if the person is more than 18 or not.

```
entry_age = 20
if entry_age >= 18:
    print("You have the minimum required age to join the golf club.")

You have the minimum required age to join the golf club.
```

Python will check to see if the value of the variable entry_age is bigger than or equal to 18. If it is, Python will execute the print statement that is indented in the code. Indentation has the same role to play in the if statements as it does in the for loops. All the indented lines that follow the if statement must be executed if the test passes. The entire block of the indented lines will be ignored if your test does not pass.

You may have multiple lines of code that you need in the block after the execution of the if statement. I will now add another line of code. Let us see how it will change the code.

```
entry_age = 20
if entry_age >= 18:
    print("You have the minimum required age to join the golf club.")
    print("Have you submitted your application to join the club?")

You have the minimum required age to join the golf club.
Have you submitted your application to join the club?
```

The conditional test passes. As both print statements are indented, both are printed logically. If you change the value to less than 18, the program will produce no output at all.

if-else Statements

You will more often need to take one action upon passing one conditional test and another action in the other cases. The if-else syntax will make it extremely possible. The if-else block is extremely similar to the if statement. The only difference is that the else statement allows you to define a set of actions or a single action that should be executed whenever a particular conditional test fails.

I will display the same message here, but I will add a new message for the person who cannot join the club.

```
entry_age = 17
if entry_age >= 18:
    print("You have the minimum required age to join the golf club.")
    print("Have you submitted your application to join the club?")
else:
    print("I am sorry, you are not old enough to join our golf club.")
    print("Please file your application when you are 18 years old.")

I am sorry, you are not old enough to join our golf club.
Please file your application when you are 18 years old.
```

If the conditional test had passed, the first block of code would be executed. Now that the first conditional test has failed, the second one has been executed. The test returns a false value, so the second block of code is executed. As the requisite age is less than 18, the test fails, and you see the second line of statements.

The if-elif-else Chain

More often, you have to test multiple possible situations. In this kind of scenario, you have to use the if-elif-else syntax. Python will execute just one block of code in the if-elif-else chain. It will run the conditional test until one test passes. When one passes, the code linked to that test will pass. Python will skip everything else.

There are a lot of real-world situations where you need to test more than two conditions. For example, sometimes, you need to allow people of multiple ages to enter a place after scanning each of them.

The following code will test the age of different people and print a statement as to where they can enter or not.

```
entry_age = 31
if entry_age > 30:
    print("You have the minimum required age to join the golf club for the mature.")
    print("Have you submitted your application to join the club?")
elif entry_age < 18:
    print("I am sorry, you are not old enough to join our golf club.")
    print("Please file your application when you are 18 years old.")
else:
    print("You are eligible only to play golf in a restricted practice area.")
    print("Please process your application at booth no 7 and move in")
```

You have the minimum required age to join the golf club for the mature.

Have you submitted your application to join the club?

Now I will change the value and the else statement to bring them into action.

```
entry_age = 25
if entry_age > 30:
    print("You have the minimum required age
to join the golf club for the mature.")
    print("Have you submitted your
application to join the club?")
elif entry_age < 18:
    print("I am sorry, you are not old
enough to join our golf club.")
    print("Please file your application when
you are 18 years old.")
else:
    print("You are eligible only to play
golf in a restricted practice area.")
    print("Please process your application
at booth no 7 and move in")

You are eligible only to play golf in a
restricted practice area.
Please process your application at booth no
7 and move in
```

If you study the code deeply, you will realize that the code can handle whatever age number you fill in. There is a statement for each category of age. There is a message for each category of age. All you need to fill in the age number and know how you have to move on.

Another Example

You can use the if statements to find out the entry fee of a person. The following code will test different age groups and then print a message as to the fee of each age category.

```
entry_age = 18
```

```
if entry_age < 5:
    print("Your entry fee will be $1.")

elif entry_age < 18:
    print("Your entry fee will be $5.")
else:
    print("Your entry fee will be $15.")
```

Your entry fee will be $15.

Multiple elif Statements

```
entry_age = 45
if entry_age < 30:
    print("You have the minimum required age to join the golf club for the mature.")
    print("Have you submitted your application to join the club?")
elif entry_age < 18:
    print("I am sorry, you are not old enough to join our golf club.")
    print("Please file your application when you are 18 years old.")
elif entry_age < 50:
    print("You can play gold in the elite club with professional players.")
    print("Please submit the fee and move on.")

else:
    print("You are eligible only to play golf in a restricted practice area.")
    print("Please process your application at booth no 7 and move in")
```

```
You can play gold in the elite club with
professional players.
```

Please submit the fee and move on.

Let us change the value and print another elif statement.

```
entry_age = 17
if entry_age > 18:
    print("You have the minimum required age
to join the golf club for the mature.")
    print("Have you submitted your
application to join the club?")
elif entry_age < 18:
    print("I am sorry, you are not old
enough to join our golf club.")
    print("Please file your application when
you are 18 years old.")
elif entry_age < 50:
    print("You can play gold in the elite
club with professional players.")
    print("Please submit the fee and move
on.")

else:
    print("You are eligible only to play
golf in a restricted practice area.")
    print("Please process your application
at booth no 7 and move in")

I am sorry, you are not old enough to join
our golf club.
Please file your application when you are 18
years old.
```

Omitting else Block

Python doesn't always require the else block at the tail of the if-elif chain. The else block is sometimes useful. However, in some cases, the elif statement is the one that is of primary interest and benefit.

```
entry_age = 65
if entry_age < 18:
    print("I am sorry, you are not old enough to join our golf club.")
    print("Please file your application when you are 18 years old.")
elif entry_age < 30:
    print("You have the minimum required age to join the golf club for the mature.")
    print("Have you submitted your application to join the club?")
elif entry_age < 65:
    print("You can play gold in the elite club with professional players.")
    print("Please submit the fee and move on.")

elif entry_age >= 65:
    print("You are eligible only to play golf in a restricted practice area.")
    print("Please process your application at booth no 7 and move in")

You are eligible only to play golf in a restricted practice area.
Please process your application at booth no 7 and move in
```

The else block is known as a catchall statement. It will match any condition that is not matched by a specific elif or if test. It can sometimes include malicious or even invalid data as well. If you have a particular final condition that you are testing, you need to consider the elif block and eliminate the else block. This will ensure that your code will only run under correct situations.

Multiple Conditions

The if-elif-else chain is robust, and it is quite appropriate for usage when you need just a single test to pass. As soon as Python finds a test will pass, it will skip the other tests. This behavior is quite beneficial because it is quite efficient and will allow you to test a specific condition.

Sometimes, you need to check the conditions that interest you. You need to use simple if statements without any else or elif blocks. The technique makes perfect sense when multiple conditions are true, and you need to act on the condition that is True.

```
veggies = ['potato', 'tomato', 'lettuce',
'cilantro', 'cabbage', 'pumpkin']
if 'tomato' in veggies:
    print("I am adding 'tomato' to the
cart.")
if 'lettuce' in veggies:
    print("I am adding 'lettuce' to the
cart.")
if 'cabbage' in veggies:
    print("I am adding 'cabbage' to the
cart.")
if 'cilantro' in veggies:
    print("I am adding 'cilantro' to the
cart.")
```

```
    print("\nThe cart is ready. Please pay
    through credit card and check out.")
```

```
    I am adding 'tomato' to the cart.
    I am adding 'lettuce' to the cart.
    I am adding 'cabbage' to the cart.
    I am adding 'cilantro' to the cart.

    The cart is ready. Please pay through credit
    card and check out.
```

I started with the list of vegetables and kept adding my favorite to my cart. Each time I added a vegetable to the cart, a message was printed on the screen. The addition of vegetables is the first test to pass. Therefore, vegetables are added to the cart of the e-commerce grocery store.

If Statement & Lists

You can pair up if statements with lists to create amazing outputs. You can produce special values that must be treated differently from the other values inside the list. You can also look out for any special values that must be treated differently from the list's other values. You may manage efficiently changing the conditions like the availability of different items inside a restaurant across the shift. You can start to prove that the code you are writing works as you expect it to be in different conditions.

Special Items

I will continue the example of the grocery app in this section as well. I have already explained the conditional test so let navigate around to see if you can check for any special values inside the list and handle the values appropriately.

The veggies example will print a message where a vegetable is added to the cart. The code for the action should be written efficiently. I will create a list of the toppings that a customer is about to buy and add to the cart. Then I will use a loop to display a message to the user.

```
veggies = ['potato', 'tomato', 'lettuce',
'cilantro', 'cabbage', 'pumpkin']
for veggie in veggies:
    print("I am adding " + veggie + ".")

print("\nThe cart is ready. Please pay
through credit card and check out.")
```

```
I am adding potato.
I am adding tomato.
I am adding lettuce.
I am adding cilantro.
I am adding cabbage.
I am adding pumpkin.

The cart is ready. Please pay through credit
card and check out.
```

The output is quite straightforward as the code is a simple for loop. Suppose a person is shopping at the grocery app, and the store runs out of lettuce. What happens next? If you add an if statement inside the for loop, it can handle this typical situation very well.

```
veggies = ['potato', 'tomato', 'lettuce',
'cilantro', 'cabbage', 'pumpkin']
for veggie in veggies:
    if veggie == 'lettuce':
        print("We are sorry as we have run out of lettuce.")
    else:
        print("I am adding " + veggie + ".")

print("\nThe cart is ready. Please pay through credit card and check out.")
```

```
I am adding potato.
I am adding tomato.
We are sorry as we have run out of lettuce.
I am adding cilantro.
I am adding cabbage.
I am adding pumpkin.

The cart is ready. Please pay through credit card and check out.
```

This time, the code behaved differently. The code checks each requested item before it is added to the cart. The code in the first line checks if the person has requested the lettuce or some other vegetable. If the person requests lettuce, the program will print a message explaining that they have run out of lettuce. The else block at the second line of code ensures that the other vegetables the person ordered are added to the cart for check out. The output shows that each vegetable that is requested is properly handled.

You also can check if the list you are working on is empty or not. We have made an assumption about each list we have worked with. Let us assume that each list has at least one item. You can let users add information to the lists. It is quite useful to see if the list is empty before the start of the loop or not. As an example, I will check first if the list of the veggies is empty before the user adds something to the cart. If the list is empty, I will ask the user whether he likes to come back again to visit at a later time. If the list is not empty, the process will go on smoothly as it did in the previous examples.

```
veggies = []

if veggies:
    for veggie in veggies:
        print("I am adding " + veggie + ".")
    print("\nThe cart is ready. Please pay through credit card and check out.")
else:
    print("We would appreciate if you could visit at our store at a later time.")

We would appreciate if you could visit at our store at a later time.
```

I started out with an empty list of veggies. Instead of moving straight to the for loop, I quickly checked the second line of code. When the name of the list is included in the if statement, Python will return True even if the list has just one value. If veggies passes the conditional test, I will run the same for loop that I had used in the previous example. If the test fails, I will print a message asking a customer if they would like to come back again later because the store is presently empty.

Multiple Lists

People may ask for anything in the store when it is about a grocery store app. What if one customer wants fruits alongside vegetables. You may use lists and the if statement to ensure that the input makes perfect sense before you start acting on it.

```
veggies = ['strawberry', 'apple', 'peach',
'potato', 'tomato', 'lettuce', 'pumpkin',
'radish']

requested_fruits = ['strawberry', 'orange',
'apple', 'peach', 'guava']

for requested_fruit in requested_fruits:
    if requested_fruit in veggies:
        print("I am adding " +
requested_fruit + ".")
    else:
        print("We don't have " +
requested_fruit + ". We would appreciate if
you could visit at our store at a later
time.")

print("\nThe cart is ready. Please pay
through credit card and check out.")
```

I am adding strawberry.

We don't have orange. We would appreciate if you could visit at our store at a later time.

```
I am adding apple.
I am adding peach.
```

We don't have guava. We would appreciate if you could visit at our store at a later time.

The cart is ready. Please pay through credit card and check out.

In the first line of code, I defined a list of veggies. You also can use a tuple here if the grocery app has a stable list of vegetables. In the second line of code, I made a list of fruits that the users request through the app. In the third line of code, I looped through the list of requested_fruits. In the loop, I checked to see if the grocers already include each fruit into the veggies list or not. If it is, the fruit will be added to the cart. If not, the user will have a message on display through the else block. The else block will run and print a message explaining to the user which fruits are not available right now.

Chapter Six

Python Dictionaries

This chapter will walk you through Python dictionaries. These allow you to connect different pieces of information that are related to one another. You will also learn how you can access information inside the dictionary. You will also learn how you can modify the requisite information. Python dictionaries can store unlimited values. The amount of information that you can add to has no limit. Just like lists, you can create a loop through the dictionaries. You will also learn how to nest one dictionary into lists, nest lists inside dictionaries, and nest dictionaries inside dictionaries.

If you develop a good understanding of dictionaries, you can accurately create models of various real-world objects. You can create a dictionary that represents a person and stores as much information as you need about the same. You may store their name, location, age, profession, married life information, and other information. At a given time, you can create two kinds of information that may be matched up like gender and profession or name and gender. That's how you can do anything with Python dictionaries. You can create a list of cities and their capitals or a list of mountains and their heights. Everything should be in pairs. That's the top requirement.

A Dictionary

In this section, I will create a simple dictionary featuring different eatable items and their types.

```
veggie_fruit = {'apple' : 'fruit', 'radish' : 'vegetable'}

print(veggie_fruit['apple'])
print(veggie_fruit['radish'])

fruit
vegetable
```

The dictionary veggie_fruit stores the name of the fruit and vegetables and their types. The print statements at the end of the code display the information as printed below. Dictionaries may look simple, but they need practice if you want to master them. Once you know how to use them, you will be better positioned to model some real-world situations through coding.

Python dictionaries are built in the form of key-value pairs where each key has a value. If you know the key, you can access its value. The value can be anything like a list, a number, a word, or another dictionary. If it were not for the dictionaries, Python would be so popular. It is the dictionaries that allow programmers to build objects in Python. By storing information in a dictionary about a real-life object, programmers model those objects in the computer world. You have to use curly braces to enclose a dictionary and add the information in key-value pairs.

The simplest dictionary has a single key-value pair. Once a dictionary has been created, you can modify it any time with more information. There is no limit to the maximum stored information in a dictionary.

Accessing Values

It is simple to access values in a dictionary. To get a value linked to a key, you need to enter the name of a dictionary and then fill it up with the key in square brackets. The following example contains the practical example for accessing values.

```
veggie_fruit = {'apple' : 'fruit', 'radish' : 'vegetable'}

print(veggie_fruit['apple'])
print(veggie_fruit['radish'])

fruit
vegetable
```

I have accessed values by entering the keys in the print statement. This is one method to access values in a dictionary. However, to use this method effectively, you need to know what your key is. You can keep a list of keys to access the related values, and you can have unlimited key-value pairs in a dictionary. You can use the information after you access it through a print statement.

```
veggie_fruit = {'fruit' : 'apple' ,
'vegetable' : 'radish'}

buy1 = veggie_fruit['fruit']
print(buy1.title() + " is just added to your
cart.")

Apple is just added to your cart.
```

Once you have defined the dictionary, the first line of code will pull the value linked to the key fruit in the dictionary. The value goes to the variable buy1.

Dictionaries are considered dynamic structures. You can add many new key-value pairs to a specific dictionary at a given time. For example, you can add key-value pairs to the dictionary. In the following example, I will add new items to the dictionary and see how they are added and how they work.

```
veggie_fruit = {'fruit' : 'apple' ,
'vegetable' : 'radish'}
print(veggie_fruit)

veggie_fruit['fruit1'] = 'orange'
veggie_fruit['vegetable1'] = 'pumpkin'
veggie_fruit['fruit2'] = 'peach'
veggie_fruit['vegetable2'] = 'carrot'

print(veggie_fruit)

{'fruit': 'apple', 'vegetable': 'radish'}
{'fruit': 'apple', 'vegetable': 'radish',
'fruit1': 'orange', 'vegetable1': 'pumpkin',
'fruit2': 'peach', 'vegetable2': 'carrot'}
```

You can see that I added four key-value pairs to the dictionary, and then I printed the dictionary. I defined the dictionary first that I had to modify by adding new key-value pairs. I defined the keys and then the values for each pair by using the equal sign and the dictionary's name. When I printed the modified dictionary, all the new key-value pairs were added to the dictionary.

It is pertinent to note that the new key-value pairs may not match the order in which you add them. Python is not concerned about the order of the key-value pairs. The only thing it cares about is the connection that each key has with its value.

Empty Dictionary

You can start with an empty dictionary and fill it up with key-value pairs. You can add as many items to the dictionary as you want. The first step in this regard is to define the dictionary with the help of empty braces. Then you can add key-value pairs on the new lines. See the following example to learn how you can build a dictionary.

```
veggie_fruit = {}

veggie_fruit['fruit'] = 'apple'
veggie_fruit['vegetable'] = 'radish'
veggie_fruit['fruit1'] = 'orange'
veggie_fruit['vegetable1'] = 'pumpkin'
veggie_fruit['fruit2'] = 'peach'
veggie_fruit['vegetable2'] = 'carrot'

print(veggie_fruit)
```

```
{'fruit': 'apple', 'vegetable': 'radish',
'fruit1': 'orange', 'vegetable1': 'pumpkin',
'fruit2': 'peach', 'vegetable2': 'carrot'}
```

You will be using empty dictionaries when you start working with the datasets that must be supplied and filled up by the data provided by users, or when you start writing the code that will generate a great number of key-value pairs automatically.

Modification

You can easily modify a dictionary. Just write the name of the dictionary with the key inside the square brackets and the new value that you need to associate with the key.

```
veggie_fruit = {'fruit' : 'apple' ,
'vegetable' : 'radish'}
print("The fruit I have to buy is " +
veggie_fruit['fruit'] + ".")

veggie_fruit['fruit'] = 'peach'
print("The fruit I have to buy is " +
veggie_fruit['fruit'] + ".")

veggie_fruit['fruit'] = 'orange'
print("The fruit I have to buy is " +
veggie_fruit['fruit'] + ".")

The fruit I have to buy is apple.
The fruit I have to buy is peach.
The fruit I have to buy is orange.
```

I defined the dictionary. Then I changed the value that is associated with the key fruit. I did that twice. The output shows the new fruit that the buyer will buy is different from the original one.

Key-Pair Removal

When you do not need a certain piece of information that is stored in the dictionary, you can use the del statement to eliminate it from the key-value pair. The del statement requires the name of the dictionary and its related key. Let's see how we can use the del statement to remove key-value pairs from the dictionary.

```
veggie_fruit = {'fruit' : 'apple' ,
'vegetable' : 'radish', 'fruit1' : 'orange',
'vegetable1' : 'pumpkin', 'fruit2' :
'peach', 'vegetable2' : 'carrot'}
print(veggie_fruit)

del veggie_fruit['fruit']
print(veggie_fruit)

del veggie_fruit['fruit1']
print(veggie_fruit)

del veggie_fruit['fruit2']
print(veggie_fruit)



{'fruit': 'apple', 'vegetable': 'radish',
'fruit1': 'orange', 'vegetable1': 'pumpkin',
'fruit2': 'peach', 'vegetable2': 'carrot'}
```

```
{'vegetable': 'radish', 'fruit1': 'orange',
'vegetable1': 'pumpkin', 'fruit2': 'peach',
'vegetable2': 'carrot'}
{'vegetable': 'radish', 'vegetable1':
'pumpkin', 'fruit2': 'peach', 'vegetable2':
'carrot'}
{'vegetable': 'radish', 'vegetable1':
'pumpkin', 'vegetable2': 'carrot'}
```

You can see that I have deleted all the fruit key-value pairs from the dictionary. The del keyword tells Python to delete the key from your dictionary. It also removes the value that is associated with the key. The output shows that the key and its related value are deleted from the dictionary. As you can see, for each item I applied the del statement, one key-value pair got deleted from the dictionary. The only thing you need to care about is that the del statement permanently deletes a key-value pair from the dictionary. You cannot get the pair back in any case.

Similar Objects Dictionary

In this example, I will store a lot of information about a single object. For example, you can store information about a house that you need to put on sale. See how you can add multiple pieces of information about an object in one dictionary.

```
house = {'swimming pool' : 'fiber glass' ,
'bathrooms' : 5, 'bedrooms' : 6, 'gym' :
'loaded with modern equipment', 'kitchen' :
'open & furnished with cooking range', 'TV
lounge' : 'furnished with cinema-sized
screen'}
print(house)
```

```
{'swimming pool': 'fiber glass',
'bathrooms': 5, 'bedrooms': 6, 'gym':
'loaded with modern equipment', 'kitchen':
'open & furnished with cooking range', 'TV
lounge': 'furnished with cinema-sized
screen'}
```

Here is how you can create a dictionary of a house that you need to put on sale. On a similar pattern, you can create different kinds of dictionaries and use them to conduct day-to-day operations.

The dictionary has been broken down from a larger dictionary into small chunks. Each key in the dictionary denotes the name of a section of the house and its description. When you realize that you need multiple lines of information to define a dictionary, you can simply hit ENTER after one brace. Then you need to indent the next line and write the next key-value pair, followed by a comma. Once you have defined the entire dictionary, you need to fill in a closing brace on the new line of the editor. Then you must indent that line as well so that it is perfectly aligned with a set of keys inside the dictionary. You can add a comma after the final key-value pair so that you are ready to include a new key-value pair in the next line of code. Most Python editors will help you format extended lists as well as dictionaries. It is their built-in feature.

Let us see how we can use the above-mentioned dictionary in a program.

```
house = {'swimming pool' : 'fiber glass' ,
'bathrooms' : 5, 'bedrooms' : 6, 'gym' :
'loaded with modern equipment', 'kitchen' :
```

```
'open & furnished with cooking range', 'TV
lounge' : 'furnished with cinema sized
screen'}

print("The swimming pool of the house is
made of " + house['swimming pool'].title() +
".")
print("The kitchen of the house is " +
house['kitchen'].title() + ".")

The swimming pool of the house is made of
Fiber Glass.
```

The kitchen of the house is Open & Furnished With Cooking Range.

You can see that you have to break up the print statement to ensure that the code works properly. The word print is mostly shorter than the dictionaries' names, which is why it makes sense that you need to find the most appropriate spot to break up the print statement.

Looping a Dictionary

Python dictionaries are humongous stores of data. You can create a dictionary and fill it up with a few pairs or a million pairs. It is easy to navigate through a short dictionary and really hard to do that with a large dictionary. That's why when you are working with a longer dictionary, you should add a loop to the code. You can create a loop through a dictionary in several ways, like looping through all the key-value pairs or looping through only the keys or only the values.

The integration of loops into a dictionary is an easy way to handle a dictionary, especially if the dictionary belongs to a corporate firm where the data is literally in millions of key-value pairs. Looping is the only way to manage large-sized data effectively.

```
I will use the same dictionary about a
house. You can access single pieces of
information. What if you need to see
everything in the dictionary? If you want to
do that, you can use the for loop to print
all the keys and values of the dictionary.
Let us see how you can build the for loop
and print the requisite values.
house = {'swimming pool' : 'fiber glass' ,
'bathrooms' : 'maple wood flooring',
'bedrooms' : 'Iranian carpeting', 'gym' :
'loaded with modern equipment'}

for key, value in house.items():
    print("\nThe house features a " + key)
    print("Here is the description: " +
value)

The house features a swimming pool
Here is the description: fiber glass

The house features a bathrooms
Here is the description: maple wood flooring

The house features a bedrooms
Here is the description: Iranian carpeting

The house features a gym
Here is the description: loaded with modern
equipment
```

I wrote the for loop for the dictionary and passed it through the keys and values of the dictionary.

The second half of the for statement includes the names of a dictionary. This will return the list of all the key-value pairs. I have created two variables, namely key and value, to store the information about the keys and values of the dictionary. You can create other variable names as suit you.

There is another way to use the information in a dictionary. You can use the information to display a neatly formatted message.

```
house = {'swimming pool' : 'fiber glass' ,
'bathroom' : 'maple wood flooring',
'bedroom' : 'Iranian carpeting', 'gym' :
'modern equipment'}

for feature, desc in house.items():
    print("The " + feature.title() + " of
the house on sale has " + desc.title() +
".")

The Swimming Pool of the house on sale has
Fiber Glass.
The Bathroom of the house on sale has Maple
Wood Flooring.
The Bedroom of the house on sale has Iranian
Carpeting.
The Gym of the house on sale has Modern
Equipment.
```

The program iterates through key-value pairs in the dictionary. As it runs through each pair, Python keys are forwarded to a variable named 'feature.' The values are forwarded and stored in the variable named as 'desc.' The information was displayed in a neat and formatted style. Descriptive variables make it easy to write and read the code. For practice, you should change the names of variables and try your own names.

Looping Through Keys

The keys() of the dictionary allow you to create a loop only through the keys of the dictionary. This time, I will loop through the dictionary and only print the house's features, which are also the dictionary's keys.

```
house = {'swimming pool' : 'fiber glass' ,
'bathroom' : 'maple wood flooring',
'bedroom' : 'Irani carpeting', 'gym' :
'modern equipment'}

for feature in house.keys():
    print("Feature of the house: " +
feature.title() + ".")

Feature of the house: Swimming Pool.
Feature of the house: Bathroom.
Feature of the house: Bedroom.
Feature of the house: Gym.
Looping through keys of a dictionary is
considered the default behavior in Python.
Therefore, when creating a loop through a
dictionary, the following code will have the
same output as the above-mentioned code.
house = {'swimming pool' : 'fiber glass' ,
'bathroom' : 'maple wood flooring',
'bedroom' : 'Iranian carpeting', 'gym' :
'modern equipment'}
```

```
for feature in house:
    print("Feature of the house: " +
feature.title() + ".")

Feature of the house: Swimming Pool.
Feature of the house: Bathroom.
Feature of the house: Bedroom.
Feature of the house: Gym.
```

You can apply the keys() method if you think it will make your code easier to read. You have the option to access the values with the help of keys by manipulating the current key. In the following example, I will change the program to display a neat message to buyers interested in buying your house. The program will include a loop that will iterate through the features that I have packed up in the dictionary. Whenever a feature matches the requirements of a buyer, the buyer will see a message on the screen.

```
house = {'swimming pool' : 'fiber glass' ,
'bathroom' : 'maple wood flooring',
'bedroom' : 'Iranian carpeting', 'gym' :
'modern equipment'}

buyer_demand = ['bathroom', 'gym']
for feature in house.keys():
    print(feature.title())

    if feature in house:
        print("Most buyers are inquiring
about " + feature.title() + " which has "+
house[feature].title() + ".")
```

```
Swimming Pool
Most buyers are inquiring about Swimming
Pool which has Fiber Glass.
Bathroom
Most buyers are inquiring about Bathroom
which has Maple Wood Flooring.
Bedroom
Most buyers are inquiring about Bedroom
which has Iranian Carpeting.
Gym
Most buyers are inquiring about Gym which
has Modern Equipment.
```

I created a list of features that buyers are asking about to create a message to show buyers what the feature has. I also checked if the feature that the buyer is asking about is in the dictionary or not. If it is, the buyer gets a detailed message that also describes the feature to make the buying decision easier.

You can use the loops to display all the keys in perfect order. A dictionary usually maintains a formal connection between the keys and the values. However, it is unlikely that you get the items from the dictionary in a predictable order. This is not a problem because you will need to obtain the accurate value that is linked with each key. One way to get everything in perfect order is to sort out the keys as they are returned through the loop.

I will use the sorted function to bring everything in perfect order as they are returned in the loop.

house = {'swimming pool' : 'fiber glass' , 'bathroom' : 'maple wood flooring', 'bedroom' : 'Irani carpeting', 'gym' : 'modern equipment'}

```
for feature in sorted(house.keys()):
    print("You will have a " +
feature.title() + " in the house.")


You will have a Bathroom in the house.
You will have a Bedroom in the house.
You will have a Gym in the house.
You will have a Swimming Pool in the house.
```

As I created loops through the keys, I will now create loops through the values in the dictionary. If you are interested in displaying the values, you can use the values() method to return the values without keys.

```
house = {'swimming pool' : 'fiber glass' ,
'bathroom' : 'maple wood flooring',
'bedroom' : 'Iranian carpeting', 'gym' :
'modern equipment'}

print("Here is the list of values of the
dictionary: ")
for desc in house.values():
    print(desc.title())

Here is the list of values of the
dictionary:
Fiber Glass
Maple Wood Flooring
Iranian Carpeting
Modern Equipment
```

You can see that I pulled all the values in the dictionary. If you repeat some values, this code won't double-check it. This may work fine with a small bunch of values, but if the number of respondents is large, this will create incredible repetition. To confirm if each value is without repetition, you can use the set. Here is how the repetition of the code works.

```
house = {'swimming pool' : 'fiber glass' ,
'bathroom' : 'maple wood flooring',
'bedroom' : 'Iranian carpeting', 'gym' :
'modern equipment', 'kitchen' : 'modern
equipment'}

print("Here is the list of values of the
dictionary: ")
for desc in house.values():
    print(desc.title())

Here is the list of values of the
dictionary:
Fiber Glass
Maple Wood Flooring
Iranian Carpeting
Modern Equipment
Modern Equipment
```

The following code will eliminate the repetition from the code.

```
house = {'swimming pool' : 'fiber glass' ,
'bathroom' : 'maple wood flooring',
'bedroom' : 'Iranian carpeting', 'gym' :
'modern equipment', 'kitchen' : 'modern
equipment'}
```

```
print("Here is the list of values of the
dictionary: ")
for desc in set(house.values()):
    print(desc.title())
```

Here is the list of values of the
dictionary:
Fiber Glass
Iranian Carpeting
Maple Wood Flooring
Modern Equipment

Nesting

You may sometimes need to store a set of dictionaries inside a list or a list of items as one value inside a dictionary. The process is known as nesting. You can nest one set of dictionaries in a list or a list in a dictionary or a dictionary in a dictionary. Nesting is known as a robust feature of dictionaries. I will demonstrate the process in the following example.

I will create a dictionary for a battle game in the following example. The dictionary players is as under,

```
player_1 = {'gun' : 'revolver', 'enemies
gunned' : 6}
player_2 = {'gun' : 'bazooka', 'enemies
gunned' : 12}
player_3 = {'gun' : 'ak-47', 'enemies
gunned' : 3}
player_4 = {'gun' : 'shot gun', 'enemies
gunned' : 15}

players = [player_1, player_2, player_3
```

```
for player in players:
    print(player)


{'gun': 'revolver', 'enemies gunned': 6}
{'gun': 'bazooka', 'enemies gunned': 12}
{'gun': 'ak-47', 'enemies gunned': 3}
```

First of all, I created four dictionaries, where each of them represented a player in the battle game. I packed up all of them into a list, namely players. Then I created a loop through the list and printed all the values of each dictionary on the screen.

You can create a fleet of players in the game if you are looking out to build an army. Players can use this dynamic piece of code to build an army and fight a large-scale war. Let's see how it goes.

```
players = []

for player_num in range(70):
    player_army = {'gun': 'revolver',
'color': 'white', 'GPS' : 'enabled'}
    players.append(player_army)

    for player in players[:7]:
        print(player)
    print("....")

print("The total number of soldiers in the army: " + str(len(players)))

{'gun': 'revolver', 'color': 'white', 'GPS': 'enabled'}
....
```

```
{'gun': 'revolver', 'color': 'white', 'GPS':
'enabled'}
{'gun': 'revolver', 'color': 'white', 'GPS':
'enabled'}
....
{'gun': 'revolver', 'color': 'white', 'GPS':
'enabled'}
{'gun': 'revolver', 'color': 'white', 'GPS':
'enabled'}
{'gun': 'revolver', 'color': 'white', 'GPS':
'enabled'}
....
{'gun': 'revolver', 'color': 'white', 'GPS':
'enabled'}
{'gun': 'revolver', 'color': 'white', 'GPS':
'enabled'}
{'gun': 'revolver', 'color': 'white', 'GPS':
'enabled'}
{'gun': 'revolver', 'color': 'white', 'GPS':
'enabled'}
....
The total number of soldiers in the army: 70
```

At the start of the example, an empty list holds the players that should be created. The range() function will return the set of numbers. It tells Python how many times you need the loop to repeat. Each time the loop runs its course, a new player will be created. It appended each player to the list of players. I used the slice method to print the players. All the players will have the same characteristics as you define for one. Python takes each of them as a separate object, which allows you to modify the players on an individual basis.

When the comes to change the guns, you can use the for loop and the if statement.

```python
players = []

for player_num in range(0, 70):
    player_army = {'gun': 'revolver', 'color': 'white', 'GPS' : 'enabled'}
    players.append(player_army)

for player in players[0:3]:
    if player['gun'] == 'revolver':
        player['gun'] = 'machine gun'
        player['color'] = 'black'
        player['GPS'] = 'disabled'

for player in players[0:6]:
    print(player)
print("....")
```

{'gun': 'machine gun', 'color': 'black', 'GPS': 'disabled'}
{'gun': 'machine gun', 'color': 'black', 'GPS': 'disabled'}
{'gun': 'machine gun', 'color': 'black', 'GPS': 'disabled'}
{'gun': 'revolver', 'color': 'white', 'GPS': 'enabled'}
{'gun': 'revolver', 'color': 'white', 'GPS': 'enabled'}
{'gun': 'revolver', 'color': 'white', 'GPS': 'enabled'}
....

You can further add to this loop the elif block and extend its functionality. The addition of the elif block will further change the specifications of players.

```
players = []

for player_num in range(0, 70):
    player_army = {'gun': 'revolver', 'color': 'white', 'GPS' : 'enabled'}
    players.append(player_army)

for player in players[0:3]:
    if player['gun'] == 'revolver':
        player['gun'] = 'machine gun'
        player['color'] = 'black'
        player['GPS'] = 'disabled'
    elif player['gun'] == 'machine gun':
        player['gun'] = 'sten gun'
        player['color'] = 'brown'
        player['GPS'] = 'enabled'

for player in players[0:6]:
    print(player)
print("....")
```

Dictionary & Lists

Instead of filling up a dictionary into a list, it is sometimes highly useful to put the list into a dictionary. For example, we can use this feature to describe something. If we have to use a list, we can add details of an object to the list. With the help of a dictionary, a list of features of a house may just be an aspect of a house or something you have been describing.

I will store two types of information in the following dictionary. One is of the house type, and the second is of the features of that house.

```
house_sale = {
    'house' : 'mansion',
    'features' : ['swimming pool', 'tennis court', 'badminton court', 'basketball court', 'bedrooms', 'open & furnished kitchen']
    }

print("The house you have you shown your interest in is a " + house_sale['house'] + " and it has the following features: ")

for feature in house_sale['features']:
    print("\t" + feature)
```

The house you have you shown your interest in is a mansion and it has the following features:

```
swimming pool
tennis court
badminton court
basketball court
bedrooms
open & furnished kitchen
```

I started with defining the dictionary that would hold information about the house on sale. One key inside the dictionary shows the type of house. The next key 'features' contains a list that has all the features of the house. When someone shows interest in purchasing the house, the final for loop will print all the elements in the list to show what the buyer will get upon the purchase. This helps us achieve multiple purposes. When I had to access the features of the house, I simply used the key features, and the entire list was brought to life on the screen. Python simply grabs the list and prints all the values.

You can use the nesting feature of Python dictionaries any time when you need to add more information to a single key.

```
player_army = {'gun': ['revolver',
'grenade'], 'gun color': ['white', 'black'],
'GPS' : ['enabled', 'military grade']}


for feature, descriptions in
player_army.items():
    print("\n" + "Here is the detail of the
key feature of your player: " +
feature.title() + ".")
    for description in descriptions:
        print("\t" + description.title())


Here is the detail of the key feature of
your player: Gun.
    Revolver
    Grenade

Here is the detail of the key feature of
your player: Gun Color.
    White
    Black
```

```
Here is the detail of the key feature of
your player: Gps.
        Enabled
        Military Grade
```

You can see that with each key in the dictionary, I have attached a list. Each list tells us more about the key. It elaborates upon the existing information. When I looped through the dictionary, I used the name descriptions to grab each value from the dictionary because each value would be a complete list. Inside the loop, I used a for loop that ran through the details of each feature of the player. Now each feature will have all the details. You can add as many details as you want to through these lists. I will expand upon the lists in the following example to demonstrate how you can create longer lists for each value. See the following example.

```
player_army = {'gun': ['revolver',
'grenade', 'revolver', 'shot gun', 'machine
gun', 'bow', 'knife'], 'gun color':
['white', 'black', 'brown', 'yellow'], 'GPS'
: ['enabled', 'military grade']}


for feature, descriptions in
player_army.items():
    print("\n" + "Here is the detail of the
key feature of your player: " +
feature.title() + ".")
        for description in descriptions:
            print("\t" + description.title())

Here is the detail of the key feature of
your player: Gun.
        Revolver
```

```
        Grenade
        Revolver
        Shot Gun
        Machine Gun
        Bow
        Knife
```

Here is the detail of the key feature of your player: Gun Color.
```
        White
        Black
        Brown
        Yellow
```

Here is the detail of the key feature of your player: Gps.
```
        Enabled
        Military Grade
```

So, that's how you can create interactive games. Just imagine how cool your games look when the user has multiple options to display the features and descriptions of his player. It just adds more fun to your games and apps. You can do the same to the grocery app that we had been trying to build through Python in the past chapters. You can take that as a test and practice this code on the grocery app code.

You can use an if statement at the start of the for loop to see if each person has multiple guns. This is done by knowing the length of the items in the lists. If a person has multiple guns, the output can stay the game. If a person has only one, you can change the output.

A word of warning is that you don't have to nest dictionaries and lists too deeply in the code. It would make the code complex, and you will find it difficult to study and comprehend it.

You also can nest a dictionary inside a dictionary. However, this, too, makes the code complicated fast. If you have multiple users on a website and each has a unique username, you can use these usernames as keys inside the dictionary. After that, you can store the information about each user by using that dictionary as a value linked to the username. See how you can do that in the following example.

```
player_army = {'gun': {'revolver' : 'one round', 'grenade': 'four' , 'shot gun': '50 rounds', 'bow': 'classic', 'knife': 'wakanda steel'}}


for feature, description in player_army.items():
    print("\n" + "Here is the detail of the key feature of your player: " + feature.title() + ".")
    desc = description['revolver'] + " " + description['grenade']
    desc1 = description['bow']

    print("\t Details of Guns: " + desc.title())
    print("\t Details of Desserts: " + desc1.title())

Here is the detail of the key feature of your player: Gun.
```

```
            Details of Guns: One Round Four
            Details of Desserts: Classic
```

First of all, I defined the dictionary as player_army. The value associated with the keys is generally a dictionary that would include the information about each player. Python will store each key into the variable that I have created.

Chapter Seven

User Input & While Loops

Python programs are user-oriented, which means that programmers write them and use them to facilitate non-tech people. Each program solves a particular problem by doing some complex calculation etc. You may need a program to determine if a person has reached a particular age to enter the golf club. A python program can help you sort out people based on their age.

You can create a program that prompts users to enter their age. After receiving the age number, the program will display a message to the user as to whether they are eligible to join the club or not. This function is known as the input() function of Python. You have to set up the minimum age number in the program. When a user enters a number through the input() function, Python will compare that number to the one you have already fed to the program and display the message accordingly.

In this chapter, I will explain how you can use the input() function to build a program that interacts with users.

Input() Function

The input() function is quite useful because it allows you to interact directly with users through Python programs. Think about a company that is looking to automate the buying process. The input() function will let you create a program that takes input from users and reacts to that input by prompting your customers to take a certain action. The action can be buying one or more products from your e-commerce store. Let us build a program that allows users to write some text and then see the same text on their screens.

```
msg = input("This is a parrot program. Whatever you say, I will repeat.")
print(msg)

This is a parrot program. Whatever you say, I will repeat.
```

You have to fill in the input() function with a single argument. If we analyze this example, we will know that Python ran through the first line of code to display the first message to the user. The user is prompted to hit Enter button. When he enters the button, his response is stored inside a variable. In return, Python will print the output to the user. The following example will further explain how the input() function helps programmers collect data from a large user base. The input() function, in practical form, is used by corporate companies that mostly maneuver with user data to run and reform their business.

```
msg = input("I want to enter your name: ")
print("Hi " + msg + ", please submit your documents and move in the hall")
```

```
=== RESTART: C:/Users/saifia
computers/Desktop/python.py ==
I want to enter your name: John
Hi John, please submit your documents and
move in the hall
>>>
=== RESTART: C:/Users/saifia
computers/Desktop/python.py ==
I want to enter your name: Adam
Hi Adam, please submit your documents and
move in the hall
>>>
```

I have added a space to the end of my prompts right after the colon. This will separate this prompt from the user's response and make it clear where the users should enter the text.

You can choose to compose longer prompts, but you may need to edit your code and write it again if you must do that. Longer prompts must be channeled into a variable for storage. Once stored, they must be passed toward the input() function. In this way, you can create longer prompts that span over multiple lines, and you will also be able to keep the code clean even after writing complex prompts.

```
msg = input("I want to enter your name to
personalize a message for you.")
msg += "\nPlease enter your name: "

user_name = input(msg)
print("Hi " + user_name + ", please submit
your documents and move in the hall")
```

```
I want to enter your name to personalize a
message for you.

Please enter your name: John
Hi John, please submit your documents and
move in the hall
```

You can see that I have built a multiline message in this example. In the second line of code, I used += takes a string that I stored in the prompt and added the new string to the end. This prompt will now span a couple of lines with some space created after the question mark to add clarity to the code.

In this example, I will determine whether people have the required age to ride the dragon coaster.

```
msg = input("Please tell me your height so
that I can estimate whether you can ride the
coaster or not.")
msg = int(msg)

if msg >= 150:
    print("\nYou have the required height to
ride the dragon coaster!")
else:
    print("\nI am sorry. You are not tall
enough to take the ride. Come back later.")

Please tell me your height so that I can
estimate whether you can ride the coaster or
not.55

I am sorry. You are not tall enough to take
the ride. Come back later.
>>>
```

```
Let us see if the user enters the required
age.
msg = input("Please tell me your height so
that I can estimate whether you can ride the
coaster or not.")
msg = int(msg)

if msg >= 150:
    print("\nYou have the required height to
ride the dragon coaster!")
else:
    print("\nI am sorry. You are not tall
enough to take the ride. Come back later.")

Please tell me your height so that I can
estimate whether you can ride the coaster or
not.160

You have the required height to ride the
dragon coaster!
>>>
```

There is one problem with this code. If you press enter without entering the age right away, you will return an error on the display. See what type of error you will witness.

Please tell me your height so that I can estimate whether you can ride the coaster or not.

```
Traceback (most recent call last):
  File "C:/Users/saifia
computers/Desktop/python.py", line 2, in
<module>
    msg = int(msg)
```

```
ValueError: invalid literal for int() with
base 10: ''
>>>
```

You can see that I didn't enter the age and got an error in return.

While Loops

The for loops take a collection of several items and execute the code once for all items. In contrast, the while loop will run as long as a specific condition stands true. I will start from the basics. The following code will calculate numbers from 1 to 8.

```
present_num = 1
while present_num <= 8:
    print(present_num)
    present_num += 1
```

```
1
2
3
4
5
6
7
8
```

I will start counting from 1 by setting up the value at 1. Then I will let the while loop run as long as the condition is true, which means the number is less than or equal to 5. The code in the loop prints the value of the present_num and then adds 1 to the value with present_num += 1. The operator += is the shorthand for the present_num = present_num +1.

The loop will be repeated as long as the condition stands true. As 1 is less than 8, Python prints 1 and then adds 1, making the presently printed number 2. Then it goes on like that and prints numbers until 8. The programs you are using on an everyday basis are likely built-in while loops. For example, a game will need the while loop to keep going on as soon as you press the quit button. Python programs would not be fun if they ceased to run before we ask them to or would keep running after we quit them. That's why while loops appear to be quite useful.

Quit Button

You can keep a program running as long as you want to by integrating it inside the while loop. I will define the quit value and keep our program running if the user does not enter the quit value. This program is very useful for games. Just imagine a game that refuses to close. What happens if a user starts it but cannot shut it down. Would the game be a success, or will it just have a real bad end? I think the second answer is most viable. The game will not run a furlong amidst high competition because users will have to unplug their PCs to shut down the game. That's why you should not forget to add the quit feature in the while loop. It will help you control the program by letting it run as long as you want and then quitting it at will.

```
msg = "\nThis is a parrot program. Whatever you say, I will repeat it for you."
msg += "\nPlease enter 'quit' to close the program: "
```

```
msg1 = ""
while msg1 != 'quit':
    msg1 = input(msg)
    print(msg1)

=== RESTART: C:/Users/saifia
computers/Desktop/python.py ==
This is a parrot program. Whatever you say,
I will repeat it for you.
Please enter 'quit' to close the program: I
am a florist.
I am a florist.

This is a parrot program. Whatever you say,
I will repeat it for you.
Please enter 'quit' to close the program: I
love to watch UFC.
I love to watch UFC.

This is a parrot program. Whatever you say,
I will repeat it for you.
Please enter 'quit' to close the program:
quit
quit
>>>
```

You can see that I have used the program twice and then I entered quit to exit. You can use any keyword here instead of quit, and it should work just fine. I will change the keyword from quit to q to simplify and speed up the process of quitting. See how it is done.

```
msg = "\nThis is a parrot program. Whatever
you say, I will repeat it for you."
msg += "\nPlease enter 'q' to close the
program: "
```

```
msg1 = ""
while msg1 != 'q':
    msg1 = input(msg)
    print(msg1)


This is a parrot program. Whatever you say,
I will repeat it for you.
Please enter 'q' to close the program: q
q
```

When the while loop runs for the first time, the msg1 is an empty string, so Python immediately starts the loop. At msg1 = input(msg), Python will display the prompt message and then wait for the next entry by the user. Whatever is entered is immediately channeled to the msg1 and stored there. It also is printed on the screen. Then Python reevaluates the condition inside the while statement. If the user has not yet entered q, it will display the prompt message and keep the program running. When the user enters 'q' in the program, Python will stop executing the code and end the program.

There is another problem that you have to deal with. The program displays the quit message such as 'quit' or 'q' as a real message. If we can change the code, we can get rid of it. I will change the code and make sure that the word quit or alphabet q are not displayed. The user should be able to quit seeing any of these messages.

```
msg = "\nThis is a parrot program. Whatever
you say, I will repeat it for you."
msg += "\nPlease enter 'q' to close the
program: "
```

```
msg1 = ""
while msg1 != 'q':
    msg1 = input(msg)

    if msg1 != 'q':
        print(msg1)
```

```
=== RESTART: C:/Users/saifia
computers/Desktop/python.py ==
This is a parrot program. Whatever you say,
I will repeat it for you.
Please enter 'quit' to close the program:
Brazil houses largest Amazon rainforests.
Brazil houses largest Amazon rainforests.
This is a parrot program. Whatever you say,
I will repeat it for you.
Please enter 'q' to close the program:
Glaciers are packed up with the purest water
on the earth.
Glaciers are packed up with the purest water
on the earth.
This is a parrot program. Whatever you say,
I will repeat it for you.
Please enter 'quit' to close the program: q
>>>
```

Flag

The program in the previous example did several tasks while also keeping the condition true. In most complex programs, there may come times where more than one event can cause the program to stop running. This can be destructive for your code. In a game, many events can lead to the end of the game. For example, a player runs of bullets and guns. He runs out of time, or he kills all enemies. The game needs to end if any of these events occur. If potentially possible events fail to end a program, testing all the conditions inside a while statement will get complicated.

A program should run as long as the conditions are true, and you may define a variable that will determine if the program is active or not. The variable, namely flag, will act as a signal to the program. You can write the programs to run as the flag is fixed at True and then stop running when different events will set its value to false.

I will use the same program to demonstrate how you can use the flag in the code and how it will affect the program's output.

```
msg = "\nThis is a parrot program. Whatever you say, I will repeat it for you."
msg += "\nPlease enter 'q' to close the program: "

active = True
while active:
    msg1 = input(msg)

    if msg1 == 'q':
        active = False
    else:
        print(msg1)
```

```
This is a parrot program. Whatever you say,
I will repeat it for you.
Please enter 'q' to close the program: Deep-sea diving is good for mental health.
Deep-sea diving is good for mental health.
```

```
This is a parrot program. Whatever you say,
I will repeat it for you.
Please enter 'q' to close the program: q
```

The if statement in the while loop will check the value of msg1. If a user enters 'q,' the active value is set to False, and the loop stops. If the user enters any value other than q, it keeps running. You might be wondering that the output is the same as the previous example. It was meant to be like that. It would be easy to add a couple of more tests. You can display a game over message in your game when a user ends the game.

Break Statement

If you want to exit the while loop in the middle of a code, you can do that by using the break statement. It will stop right there without executing the rest of the code. The break statement will regulate the flow of the program. You can use it to control different lines of code. By using it, you will ensure that the program executes the code as per your will. I will create a new program and add the break statement to see how it works and how you can use it in your programs.

```
msg = "\nI want you to enter the names of
English literary figures."
msg += "\n(Please enter 'q' to close the
program.) "

while True:
    msg1 = input(msg)

    if msg1 == 'q':
```

```
            break
    else:
        print("I love the works of " +
msg1.title() + "!")
```

```
I want you to enter the names of English
literary figures.
(Please enter 'q' to close the program.)
John Donne
I love the works of John Donne!

I want you to enter the names of English
literary figures.
(Please enter 'q' to close the program.)
Christopher Marlowe
I love the works of Christopher Marlowe!

I want you to enter the names of English
literary figures.
(Please enter 'q' to close the program.)
Alexander Pope
I love the works of Alexander Pope!

I want you to enter the names of English
literary figures.
(Please enter 'q' to close the program.) q
```

If a loop starts with while True, it is meant to run on end until it hits upon the break statement. The loop will continue until the user enters 'q.' When Python finds 'q' in the prompt, it will activate the break statement that runs its course and stops the program from any further execution.

Continue Statement

The continue statement works with the break statement. Instead of breaking the loop, you can add the continue statement to your code and return to the start of your loop based on the conditional test results. Let see how I add the continue statement to the following program.

```
my_num = 0
while my_num < 8:
    my_num += 1
    if my_num % 2 == 0:
        continue

    print(my_num)

1
3
5
7
```

While Loops, Lists & Dictionaries

I have so far worked with just a single piece of information that users entered as input. I then printed that input on the screen of the interpreter. Next time through the while loop, I will receive an input value that would respond to the same. To keep track of different information and users, I will have to use different dictionaries and lists to pair up with the while loops. The for loop does not work well with dictionaries and lists.

Moving Items

I will form two lists of graduated students and ungraduated students from a university. After the verification process of students, I will shift students from the ungraduated students to graduated students. The While loop will help pull students from the ungraduated list to the graduated list. The code for the program takes the following shape.

```
ungraduated_students = ['john', 'abe',
'jasmine', 'asim']
graduated_students = []

while ungraduated_students:
    my_students = ungraduated_students.pop()

    print("I am verifying the students'
degrees: " + my_students.title())
    graduated_students.append(my_students)

    print("\nHere is the list of the
graduated students:")
    for graduated_student in
graduated_students:
        print(graduated_student.title())

I am verifying the students' degrees: Asim

Here is the list of the graduated students:
Asim
I am verifying the students' degrees:
Jasmine

Here is the list of the graduated students:
Asim
```

```
Jasmine
I am verifying the students' degrees: Abe

Here is the list of the graduated students:
Asim
Jasmine
Abe
I am verifying the students' degrees: John

Here is the list of the graduated students:
Asim
Jasmine
Abe
John
```

I started with a list of ungraduated students, and then using the while loop, I shifted all the students from the ungraduated list to the graduated list. I did this one by one. The while loop helped me flawlessly achieve this objective.

Removing Instances

You can use the remove() function to remove different values from the list. You can remove different instances of a single value from a list by using the while loop. The while loop will find each instance and kick it out of the loop.

```
fruits = ['apple', 'peach', 'guava',
'apple', 'melon', 'apple', 'grapes']
print(fruits)

while 'apple' in fruits:
    fruits.remove('apple')
```

```
print(fruits)

['apple', 'peach', 'guava', 'apple',
'melon', 'apple', 'grapes']
['peach', 'guava', 'melon', 'grapes']
```

I created a list that contained different names of fruits. After I had printed the list, Python entered the while loop because it found the value 'apple' at least once. When Python entered the loop, it removed the first instance and returned to the while loop. Then it once again entered the while line and removed another instance. It kept repeating the circle until it removed the last instance of the word 'apple.'

Filling Up Dictionaries

You can create an empty dictionary and fill it up with user input as you proceed with the program's functioning. You create prompts for as much input as you need with the help of the while loop. Let us create a program that receives user input and stores it in a dictionary. I will store the data that I will gather inside a dictionary.

```
data = {}

survey = True

while survey:
    name = input("\nPlease enter your name. ")
    datum = input("What is your favorite tourist destination? ")
    data[name] = datum
```

```
    repeat = input("Would like to pass on
the survey paper to another person?")
    if repeat == 'no':
        survey = False
print("\n------Here are the results of the
survey------")
for name, datum in data.items():
    print(name + " loves to visit " + datum
+ ".")

Please enter your name. John
What is your favorite tourist destination?
Greece
Would you like to pass on the survey paper
to another person?yes

Please enter your name. Adam
What is your favorite tourist destination?
Italy
Would you like to pass on the survey paper
to another person?yes

Please enter your name. Jasmine
What is your favorite tourist destination?
Spain
```

Would you like to pass on the survey paper to another person?no

```
------Here are the results of the survey----
--
John loves to visit Greece.
Adam loves to visit Italy.
Jasmine loves to visit Spain.
```

Chapter Eight

Python Functions

This chapter will walk you through Python functions that are blocks of code specifically designed to perform a particular job. When you perform a specific task defined as a function, you will call the name of that function responsible for it. If you have to perform the same task more than one time in the same program, you need not write the same code over and over again. All you need is to call that function that handles the job, and Python will execute the entire code associated with that function. You will find that the use of functions will make the programs easier to handle.

This chapter will walk you through the information you need to write functions that display information and process data. There may be many other key jobs that your functions may perform. I will explain how you can store functions in separate files known as modules to help organize the major program files.

```
def greetings():
    print("Hello, how are you dear?")

greetings()
```

```
Hello, how are you dear?
```

This is an example of a simple function. The example explains the structure of the function. The first line uses the def keyword to inform Python that a function is being defined. This is a function definition that tells Python what the name of the function is. Here the name is greetings(). There is no extra information needed at the moment to ensure the smooth flow of the function. Its job is merely to print greetings for the function. That's why the parentheses are empty. The definition ends on a colon.

The indented lines make up the body of the function. The line that contains the print statement is the real line of code in the entire structure. When you want Python to execute the code, you simply write a function call by writing the function's name and adding to it the parentheses.

Once you have created a function, you can pass on different snippets of information to that function. I will use the same function and pass on different pieces of information to see how the function receives them and uses them in the code.

```
def greetings(yourname):
    print("Hello, " + yourname.title() + " how are you? Have some tea!")

greetings('Jasmine')
greetings('Johnny')
greetings('Stark')

Hello, Jasmine how are you? Have some tea!
```

```
Hello, Johnny how are you? Have some tea!
Hello, Stark how are you? Have some tea!
```

Arguments & Parameters

When I passed the names to the functions, I used the parameter feature of the function. The name is the parameter of the function. The value that I filled into the function when I made the function call is an example of the function argument. You must pass information to the function in the form of arguments and parameters. Some people interchangeably treat parameters and arguments. However, this is not appropriate. You can pass on multiple parameters to a function. Also, you can use several ways to do that. One of the top methods is to use positional arguments that need to be in a coherent order in which the parameters were written.

When you make a function call, Python needs to match arguments inside the function call with one parameter in the definition of that function. The simplest way is usually based on the order in which you have provided the arguments. The values that you have matched up in this way are labeled as positional arguments. See the following example.

```
def desc_pet(pet_kind, name):
    print("\nOur house has a " + pet_kind + ".")
    print("\nWe have named our " + pet_kind + " as " + name + ".")

desc_pet('eagle', 'Gabriel')

Our house has a eagle.
```

```
We have named our eagle as Gabriel.
```

The output of the code describes a pet with name and kind. You can make multiple function calls to describe more than one animal through the same function. You don't have to write new code for that. All you will do is pass on new arguments to the parameters that we have defined. See the following example to understand thoroughly.

```
def desc_pet(pet_kind, name):
    print("\nOur house has a " + pet_kind + ".")
    print("\nWe have named our " + pet_kind + " as " + name + ".")

desc_pet('eagle', 'Gabriel')
desc_pet('tiger', 'John')
desc_pet('cat', 'David')


Our house has a eagle.

We have named our eagle as Gabriel.

Our house has a tiger.

We have named our tiger as John.

Our house has a cat.

We have named our cat as David.
```

Multiple function calls are an efficient way to get the work done. You can easily produce multiple results with the same code.

Well, you might have thought that functions are easy. However, this is not the case if you miss out on the order of the arguments. Python does not differentiate between the right and the wrong orders. It just takes an argument and connects it with the parameter. If you write the arguments in the wrong order, it is highly likely that you produce the wrong output and ends up getting frustrated. See how a wrong order can ruin your code.

```
def desc_pet(pet_kind, name):
    print("\nOur house has a " + pet_kind + ".")
    print("\nWe have named our " + pet_kind + " as " + name + ".")

desc_pet('Gabriel', 'eagle')
desc_pet('John', 'tiger')
desc_pet('David', 'cat')

Our house has a Gabriel.

We have named our Gabriel as eagle.

Our house has a John.

We have named our John as tiger.

Our house has a David.

We have named our David as cat.
```

However, Python also offers a solution to this problem. If you are worried about the order of the arguments, you can use keyword arguments. A keyword argument is like a name-value pair that you pass on to a function. You should link the name and the value inside the argument so that there is little confusion left when you pass on the argument.

```
def desc_pet(pet_kind, name):
    print("\nOur house has a " + pet_kind + ".")
    print("\nWe have named our " + pet_kind + " as " + name + ".")

desc_pet(name = 'Gabriel', pet_kind = 'eagle')
desc_pet(name = 'John', pet_kind = 'tiger')

Our house has a eagle.

We have named our eagle as Gabriel.

Our house has a tiger.

We have named our tiger as John.
```

Default Values

Python also takes in some default values. You can define the value of your choice to default values for each parameter. If you fail to provide arguments to a function call, it will pick up the default values and produce the results. This helps in multiple function calls where you can miss out on one call and then let the function use the default values to finish the function call. In the following example, I will define the default values for a function and use them in the function call.

```
def desc_pet(pet_kind = 'peacock', name = 'Rosie'):
```

```
        print("\nOur house has a " + pet_kind + 
".")
        print("\nWe have named our " + pet_kind 
+ " as " + name + ".")

desc_pet(name = 'Gabriel', pet_kind = 
'eagle')
desc_pet()
desc_pet(name = 'Lucy')
desc_pet(name = 'John', pet_kind = 'tiger')
```

Our house has a eagle.

We have named our eagle as Gabriel.

Our house has a peacock.

We have named our peacock as Rosie.

Our house has a peacock.

We have named our peacock as Lucy.

Our house has a tiger.

We have named our tiger as John.

If you do not fill in the default values and still you make an empty function call, you will receive an error. Here is how the error looks like.

```
def desc_pet(pet_kind , name):
    print("\nOur house has a " + pet_kind + 
".")
    print("\nWe have named our " + pet_kind 
+ " as " + name + ".")
```

```
desc_pet()

Traceback (most recent call last):
  File "C:\Users\saifia
computers\Desktop\python.py", line 4, in
<module>
    desc_pet()
TypeError: desc_pet() missing 2 required
positional arguments: 'pet_kind' and 'name'
>>>
```
You can use a function inside a loop.
```
def formatted_nm(ft_nm, lt_nm):
    """This code will return the complete
name in a neatly formatted manner."""
    complete_name = ft_nm + ' ' + lt_nm
    return complete_name.title()
# This is an infinite loop!
while True:
    print("\nPlease tell the name:")
    fst_name = input("My first name: ")
    lst_name = input("My last name: ")

    the_formatted_name =
formatted_nm(fst_name, lst_name)
    print("\nHello, how are you, " +
the_formatted_name + "!")

Please tell the name:
My first name: Eva
My last name: Jasmine

Hello, how are you, Eva Jasmine!

Please tell the name:
My first name: John
My last name: Adams
```

```
Hello, how are you, John Adams!

Please tell the name:
My first name:
```

By looking at the code, you can tell that the code is not going to end easily. That's why we need to add the break statement to kill the code whenever you need to. The break statement will help you exit the while loop whenever you need to.

```
def formatted_nm(ft_nm, lt_nm):
    """This code will return the complete
name in a neatly formatted manner."""
    complete_name = ft_nm + ' ' + lt_nm
    return complete_name.title()
# This is an infinite loop!
while True:
    print("\nPlease tell the name:")
    print("(please enter 'q' to exit the loop.)")

    fst_name = input("My first name: ")
    if fst_name == 'q':
        break

    lst_name = input("My last name: ")
    if lst_name == 'q':
        break


    the_formatted_name = formatted_nm(fst_name, lst_name)
    print("\nHello, how are you, " + the_formatted_name + "!")
```

```
============= RESTART: C:\Users\saifia
computers\Desktop\python.py =============

Please tell the name:
(please enter 'q' to exit the loop.)
My first name: John
My last name: q
>>>
============= RESTART: C:\Users\saifia
computers\Desktop\python.py =============

Please tell the name:
(please enter 'q' to exit the loop.)
My first name: John
My last name: Adams

Hello, how are you, John Adams!

Please tell the name:
(please enter 'q' to exit the loop.)
My first name: q
>>>
```

I produced two outputs to show how you can end at two different points because I have added two break statements to the code.

Chapter Nine

Classes

Python classes are all about object-oriented programming. By using the classes, you can create objects that are modeled on real-life objects. When you write a class, you define the behavior of the entire category of objects that you have to model.

Each object in a class is equipped with a behavior. You can give each object a bunch of unique traits as per your will. You may be amazed at how well you can model some real-world situations in your codes. The process of creating an object inside of a class is called instantiation.

Creating Eagle Class

In the following code, I will show you how you can create an eagle class in Python. I will add some instances to the class and make the object perform some key functions.

```
class Bald_eagle():
    """I am modeling an eagle in the
following code."""
```

```python
    def __init__(self, eagle_name, eagle_age, eagle_color):
        """Here I am initializing the name and age attributes of the eagle."""
        self.eagle_name = eagle_name
        self.eagle_age = eagle_age
        self.eagle_color = eagle_color
    def sitting(self):
        """Now I am Simulating the eagle to sit on the top of the mountain."""
        print(self.eagle_name.title() + " is sitting at the moment on the top of the mountain.")
    def flying(self):
        """The eagle is now flying through the clouds."""
        print(self.eagle_name.title() + " is flying across the clouds!")
    def preying(self):
        """The eagle is now attacking a rabbit."""
        print(self.eagle_name.title() + " is now preying upon a wild rabbit along the bank of a lake!")

eagle1 = Bald_eagle('Tin Tin', 5, 'brown')
print("The name of my eagle is " + eagle1.eagle_name.title() + ".")
print("The age of the eagle is " + str(eagle1.eagle_age) + ".")
print("The color of the eagle is " + eagle1.eagle_color.title() + ".")
eagle1.sitting()
eagle1.flying()
eagle1.preying()
```

```
eagle2 = Bald_eagle('Teem', 6, 'brown')
print("The name of my eagle is " +
eagle2.eagle_name.title() + ".")
print("The age of the eagle is " +
str(eagle2.eagle_age) + ".")
print("The color of the eagle is " +
eagle2.eagle_color.title() + ".")
eagle2.sitting()
eagle2.flying()
eagle2.preying()

eagle3 = Bald_eagle('Sim', 7, 'black')
print("The name of my eagle is " +
eagle3.eagle_name.title() + ".")
print("The age of the eagle is " +
str(eagle3.eagle_age) + ".")
print("The color of the eagle is " +
eagle3.eagle_color.title() + ".")
eagle3.sitting()
eagle3.flying()
eagle3.preying()

The name of my eagle is Tin Tin.
The age of the eagle is 5.
The color of the eagle is Brown.
Tin Tin is sitting at the moment on the top
of the mountain.
Tin Tin is flying across the clouds!
Tin Tin is now preying upon a wild rabbit
along the bank of a lake!
The name of my eagle is Teem.
The age of the eagle is 6.
The color of the eagle is Brown.
Teem is sitting at the moment on the top of
the mountain.
Teem is flying across the clouds!
```

```
Teem is now preying upon a wild rabbit along
the bank of a lake!
The name of my eagle is Sim.
The age of the eagle is 7.
The color of the eagle is Black.
Sim is sitting at the moment on the top of
the mountain.
Sim is flying across the clouds!
Sim is now preying upon a wild rabbit along
the bank of a lake!
```

You can see that I have created three objects from the same class. Technically, it means that I have created three different objects from the same class.

Conclusion

Now that you have made it to the end of the book, I am sure that you have been equipped with Python programming basics. Python programming can be a piece of cake if you master the basics like data types, loops, functions, conditionals, etc. Once you have aced these, you can go on to master object-oriented programming, of which I have given you a slight glimpse in this book.

The best course of action onward is to take your computer and practice the codes as much as you can so that you get familiar with different types of outputs, errors, and other complications. Unless you get familiar with the complications and errors, you are unlikely to make sufficient progress. It is the errors and frustratingly wrong outputs that compel programmers to delve deeper into the code and understand why something got wrong in the first place.

Once you start questioning yourself as to what happens to something in the first place, you can consider yourself a programmer. Don't worry if you don't get it right and if things take time to be corrected. This means you are learning new codes and new techniques. Also, the most important is not to stop experimenting. The more you try new methods and produce more examples, the better you will learn Python.

References

Decorators with parameters in Python. (2021, July 7). GeeksforGeeks. https://www.geeksforgeeks.org/decorators-with-parameters-in-python/?ref=lbp

Python data types. (n.d.). W3Schools Online Web Tutorials. https://www.w3schools.com/python/python_datatypes.asp

Python Tuples. (n.d.). W3Schools Online Web Tutorials. https://www.w3schools.com/python/python_tuples.asp

Python while loop. (2021, May 14). GeeksforGeeks. https://www.geeksforgeeks.org/python-while-loop/?ref=lbp

Taking input from console in Python. (2020, November 27). GeeksforGeeks. https://www.geeksforgeeks.org/taking-input-from-console-in-python/?ref=lbp

Lightning Source UK Ltd.
Milton Keynes UK
UKHW020656010722
405240UK00009B/518